Basic Guide to the Great Dane

*Written by breeders
who know the breed...
For those who are interested in
learning more about the
Great Dane*

To all those who have challenged me: "Here's to you......."

Printed in the United States of America

ISBN 0-932045-11-1
Library of Congress Catalog Card Number 96-96110

Front Cover: **Scarbrough Fair's Contessa**
Owned by Arlene Scarbrough
Scarbrough Fair Great Danes,
Atlanta, Georgia — See Page 64

Back Cover: **WYSIWYG Blue Star's Wülfgar**
Owned by Mark and Sheila Lobdell,
Bred by Teresa La Brie, WYSIWYG Great Danes
Norwich, NY — See Page 64

The *Basic Guide to the Great Dane* is written from information collected about the breed from some of the top breeders in the nation. In this way the material presented is not only breed specific, but is an overview of the breed as seen by many kennels and breeders, not the breed as viewed by a single individual and limited to their experiences. We would like to thank the following people for their help in putting this project together.

Michael R. Zervas - Managing Editor
Stephen W. Jones - Project Editor
Trevor A. Shand - Production Coordinator

And a special thank you for the tremendous help we received from the following owners, breeders and of course, lovers of the Great Dane.

CONTRIBUTING AUTHORITIES IN NO PARTICULAR ORDER:

Kevin & Charlotte Cavell	Bill & Betty Lewis	Clare Lincoln
Dr. Swift	Dr. Colin Hagan	Robert E. Layne
Gisela Wood	Arlene Scarbrough	Jill Swedlow
Linda Arndt	Janette & Roy Robinson	Nancy Simmons
Derek & Elise Allison	Jackie White	Bob Herd
Colleen Leahy	Betty Thomas	Anita S. Brown
Susan Reiter	Teresa LaBrie	Louis G. Bond
Willliam & Laurie Crossman	Sandy Tombari	Sue & Steve Mahany
Henley Dodge	Melissa L. Dreyer	Jodie & Bud Keim
Betty Lou Wood	Holly Bennett	Chuck & Willie Crawford
Susan Davis Shaw	Lori & Tim Keefe	Sharon Ann Day
Stephanie Gallups	Tom & Barbara Lewellen	Jill Ferrera
J.B. & Sandy Britts	Patricia Thurow	Peg Billings
Jean M. Bell	Glenn & Gloria Bearss	Raymond Goldstone
Joan Byas	Great Dane Club of America	Jerome & Olivia Seehof
Bonnie & Gayle Klompstra	Patricia Ciampa	Jeanette Pickett
Tonie Gerhardt	Edward Lyons, Jr.	

Your years of knowledge and interest in the breed has not only made this book possible, but insures the future of the Great Dane.

HOW TO USE THE BASIC GUIDE BREED SERIES

This series of books is written for the person who is investigating the breed for a possible pet; for the person who has decided on a Great Dane and wants to know how to find a good breeder and what to ask; for the person who has just bought a Great Dane who wants to know what to expect and how to train it; and for the person who owns a Great Dane and wants to know more about the breed and how closely his or her dog resembles current champions of the breed. These books are also a *beginning point* for those who want to know what else they can do with their dogs.

The Basic Guide to the Great Dane takes a unique approach. Instead of being the opinion of one kennel, with one style of dog and one view of the breed, we have interviewed many breeders and have pooled their vast knowledge and interest in the breed to create an overview as **NO OTHER BREED BOOK** provides. The knowledge and experience reflected here are not limited to a single person.

This series is truly educational for the reader. In many places, where breeders have given us conflicting information, we have pooled that information, making note that there is dispute within the breed and indicating that further discussion with individual breeders is advisable.

OUR TWO SPECIAL SECTIONS

The **HALL OF FAME** section not only puts new people in contact with breeders of top quality animals as a place to start their search, but it also gives the reader a chance to see the different styles within the breed. By carefully studying the pedigrees provided, it is a start in understanding the relation of the pedigree to the individual dog - the cornerstone upon which breeds and breed registries are built. If you already own a Great Dane, you might enjoy looking through this section and comparing your dog and its pedigree with those who have been achievers in the world of dogs!

Finally, the **SHOPPING ARCADE** section puts readers in contact with some of the fine businesses whose products relate to dogs and to Great Danes in particular. For those of us who show dogs on a regular basis, we meet some of these fine specialty businesses every week. For those who do not attend such events, the Shopping Arcade section provides a chance to find these quality products which will make excellent gifts for the breed lover, additions to your home, or products to help you raise a happy, healthy dog.

We sincerely hope you find this book informative and entertaining and that you have as much fun reading it as we have had producing it, and as much fun as our breeders have had producing fine quality dogs for so many years.

BEFORE YOU BUY A DOG

1) Decide WHAT YOU WANT THE DOG TO DO. Evaluate your home and lifestyle and how a dog should fit into your life.

2) Look at different breeds and decide what breed is best for you and your home.

3) Realize that there are differences in style and temperament within each breed. Different breeders select their breeding stock based on different criteria. Use the Hall of Fame to help you see the differences among dogs and kennels.

4) Find a breeder who produces dogs which will fit your needs. Ask questions which will insure that the dog you buy will be right for you by finding a breeder who places importance on the qualities which are important to you.

5) Be sure to ask the breeder the right questions for that particular breed and be prepared for what the breeder will want to ask you.

With this in mind, your decision will be an informed one and the dog you buy will be a welcome addition to your family for years to come.

Table of Contents

Section I

Section II

Great Danes are gentle giants and have been used as Junior Showmanship dogs because of their wonderful temperaments. However, their size puts them at a disadvantage in a small ring when they must compete against smaller dogs. In Junior Showmanship the ability of the young handler is judged rather than the quality of the dog, and competitors of all breeds will be in the ring together. Pictured here is Junior Handler, Melissa Sterling.

INTRODUCTION

We are often asked, "Why buy a purebred dog?" Certainly there are some wonderful, loving and even talented mutts. But have you ever owned a dog, or known a mutt you admired and been frustrated in trying to locate another like him?

Centuries ago, people kept dogs for pets, for working partners in their fields and with their flocks, as hunting companions, and for protection of the family. As dogs began to diversify, people noticed certain dogs were better at one thing than others. People liked the looks of one dog over another, or found that one had better instincts in certain areas than another. Dogs in one geographic area began to look alike from interbreeding within a small population, and people who lived in other areas came to buy such dogs when they wanted a certain characteristic or look. Thus dog breeds began to evolve. The breeds were based on predictability of looks and performance in a dog from a certain area or gene pool.

Breeders, and later field or kennel clubs began to keep records of individuals. This recording of the gene pool is a second step in creating a breed. Without such record keeping, a breed will change and lose characteristics. Again, it is insurance that a puppy will grow to look and act like certain other individuals.

Finally, people wrote descriptions of the breed. At first these were simply descriptions of certain dogs which impressed the author on a hunt, or in traveling. These descriptions are our earliest written standards. Later, breeders banded together to form breed clubs and they wrote a detailed, collective description of the breed for others to follow. Careful breeders who studied the standard, thought about the original purpose of the breed, and were concerned about health and temperament, continued the breed.

The value of a breed, and a registration to record it, is that a buyer of a puppy can predict what it will look like when it is grown up, what its talents and temperament will be and how well it will fit a living situation. If we owned and raised nothing but crossbreeds, or if you simply got a cute puppy from the dog pound, you would have no way of knowing what you might be sharing your home and your life with for the next twelve to fourteen years!

And there is a certain pride of ownership in a stylish, quality dog. It does not take an experienced eye to tell the difference between a fine antique and a fake, between a fine luxury car and a clunker. To say that there is no reason to get a purebred dog instead of a mutt is like saying that a Geo will get you there just as well as a Cadillac. Both fill the same job of taking the driver from one place to another, but the pride of ownership is entirely different. It does not take training to recognize quality in an animal. It is manifested in the way the dog comes together, the way the over-all animal pleases the eye, the attitude and presence - self confidence - of the dog. Good breeding, soundness, and aptitude of purpose are a source of pleasure. If you *divide the cost of the average puppy from a good breeder, by the life span of the dog, you will be paying less than fifty dollars a year, or about four dollars a month for the pleasure of an animal that will be recognizable as his breed, serve the purpose for which he was bred, and have the health and temperament that will make him fit your family and life-style.*

In this way, you will find an animal that will be a good fit, one that will share your home and your love for a lifetime, instead of getting a puppy that grows into an individual you cannot live with, and one which causes frustration and stress.

Breeders find that new owners who take this kind of time to locate a puppy are far more likely to be satisfied with their new family member. They are more likely to realize what care of that breed will entail, will be more likely to provide a good home, and far less likely to take it to the pound or otherwise get rid of the animal.

So, take the time to do your homework about the breed. A dog is not only what it looks like, but how easy it is to live with in a given situation. No breed is perfect for everyone. Find out what questions to ask for that particular breed, locate breeders, and take your time to find a puppy or adult dog which will meet your needs. For those purposes, we hope these <u>*BASIC GUIDE*</u> *books will be helpful.*

HISTORY

*T*he people of ancient Greece, land of Plato, Aristotle, Virgil and Homer, valued all that was proud and noble. They valued beauty and strength in mind and body. In this ancient cradle of civilization was bred a dog, a giant fit to match the warrior's pride and nobility. This dog, known as the Molossian Hound, was bred in the Molossia district of Epirus. In Mesopotamia, the Assyrian Giant Hunting Dogs moved across the fields. These huge animals, alert and strong with short, smooth coats, were powerful allies of their human hunting companions. In Rome, Roman emperors watched in the Colosseum while dogs fought bears, bulls and even tigers. These dogs, known as Giant Fighting Hounds, could bring the crowds to their feet with their valor and strength.

The dogs depicted in Assyrian engravings from as far back as 2000 BC closely resemble the Great Dane we know today. The Assyrians were a highly cultured race. Their manufactured goods, made of gold, silver and ivory, were traded widely, and it is likely that they exported their dogs through the same channels. Excavations from Russia, Poland and throughout middle Germany have revealed drawings, coins and sculpture featuring dogs with anatomical construction very close to that of modern Danes. An article published by the Great Dane Club of Italy in 1929 cites the earliest written description of a dog resembling the Great Dane to be a Chinese work written in 1121 BC. On friezes, coins, carvings and tablets the breed we call the Great Dane is depicted and described as looking much like it looks today.

Throughout its long history, the Great Dane has been known by many different names. Exactly why the breed came to be referred to as the "Great Dane" in America (of all the many names applied to the breed throughout history) is a mystery. The "Great Dane" did not originate in Denmark, as might be expected from the name. The name "Great Dane" comes from an old French designation, *grand Danois,* or big Danish. By some of the best sources, the French were also calling the breed *dogue allemand* or German Mastiff, at about the same time. Another name popularly applied to the breed is *Deutsche dogge,* the term by which the breed is known in Germany today. Certainly the breed was well known in Germany, and German fanciers led the world in developing the breed into that which is known today. Throughout history German breeders have bred some of the best specimens, and it would seem to have made more sense to have used that country in the name rather than Denmark.

The breed known as the Molossian Hound, which the Phoenicians had taken to Britain in the sixth century AD, began the root stock of the British Great Dane. Developing throughout the time the Romans occupied Great Britain, many of the dogs who found their place with the Roman legions and in the fighting rings which entertained the masses, came from stock sent back to Rome from Great Britain. In order to procure the best specimens possible, the Roman Emperor had a special official called the *procurator Cynogie*, who lived in Winchester, which was known at that time as the "City of Dogs."

Like all ancient breeds which developed over time, the Great Dane had a distinct purpose. He was a hunting dog. Because of his size, he was used against large or fierce game. In

Germany, he was used against the European wild boar, one of the most savage, swift and powerful game animals on the continent. Wealthy lords and princes formed large hunting packs of dogs similar to Great Danes which became known as Boar Hounds. Many fine prints and illustrations from Medieval Europe depict wild boar hunts in progress. Boar Hounds were crossed with English Hounds throughout the fifteenth and sixteenth century, but this importation and crossbreeding stopped by the seventeenth and eighteenth century, when homebred German dogs were preferred. The German breeders had developed a superdog to attack its prey. Today, the Argentine Dogo, a very similar descendent of the Great Dane, is still used to hunt boar throughout Argentina and South America.

The dog's purpose in turn influenced how the breed developed. The Greyhound and the Mastiff were heavily introduced into the breed to increase both speed and size.

In the German courts throughout the seventeenth century, the largest and best dogs were called "Kammerhunde" or *Chamber Dogs.* They wore beautifully gilded collars. The second best were known as "Leibhunde" or *Life Dogs.* They wore collars with a silver finish. Class distinctions, even between dogs, were a common part of life in the European courts of the time.

The steady popularity of the Great Dane is evident throughout history. They are mentioned by many early writers, such as Holinshed (1560), Camden (1568), Ware (1654), and Evelyn (1660-1670). Alexander Pope (1688-1744) owned a Dane which was his faithful companion for many years and the dog became famous through his master's writings. Descriptions of many of the early Danes mentioned silver-fawns, very probably gray. A pair, Hannibal and Princess, described as "wild boar hounds," were presented to Her Royal Highness the Duchess of York in 1807.

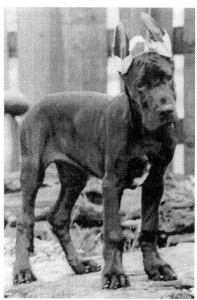

Ears need to be cropped when the pup is young and need care and taping for several months.

Like most breeds, the description and standardization of the Great Dane did not begin until the nineteenth century, but the Great Dane was one of the first breeds to have breeding records kept in England. One dog, born in 1881, carried a pedigree that went back fourteen generations to a dog born in 1830. This kind of breeding record was very unusual, as most breeds did not develop their genealogical record keeping until well into the second half of the nineteenth century. The Great Dane Club of Germany adopted its first standard, or official description of the ideal specimen, in 1891. The Standard was followed in the foundation of the Great Dane Club of England in 1885, and one in Chicago in 1889. The Great Dane Club of America was the fourth breed club to affiliate with the American Kennel Club. Its bylaws were passed in 1891.

Around the turn of the century, King Edward VII, who was then Prince of Wales, expressed his wish that the cropping of ears, which had universally been done with the breed for centuries, should stop. Many fanciers were disappointed in the look of the dog without cropped ears and the edict proved to be a setback for the breed when several breeders and enthusiasts lost interest. When interest in the breed was revived, a small group of dedicated breeders began to breed Great Danes with smaller, more attractive ears. To this day, ear cropping is not done in England. A lengthy quarantine on dogs coming into England means few dogs are imported, so cropped ears are seldom seen on the British Isles. One of our fanciers said she has noticed several movies and television shows, including *Murder She Wrote,*—with scenes which supposedly take place in England—featuring cropped Great Danes. To anyone who is familiar with the breed, cropped ears are a flashing sign that the scene was actually filmed in the United States.

Great Danes were imported into the United States in the middle 1800s. One of the earliest Danes was a black dog named "Turk," which was owned by the family of Colonel William Cody, the famous "Buffalo Bill." The dog looked after the five Cody children, served as a guard dog, spotted game and served the family well as a constant companion. At least two incidents are written about his valor in saving family members, and a painting of the family with Turk is in the Buffalo Bill Historical Association museum. When Buffalo Bill became famous, he owned several Great Danes, which traveled with him and the Wild West Show.

Great Danes were not shown in the United States under their present name until the late nineteenth century. Eleven Great Danes were shown in the Philadelphia Grand National Show in 1877 under the name Ulm Dogs. In 1878 they were shown in Westminister under the name Siberian.

The fashionable crowds of the 1880s saw the Great Dane at the American Institute Building at the Exposition in New York, but the temperament of the dogs was so poor that several fights ensued among them. The breed was barred from competition in the United States for seven years.

American breeders set about to improve temperaments and eliminate the unmanageable traits. Over the next twenty years they were remarkably successful, and the breed entered this century with the characteristic gentle nature it exhibits today. The original protective traits are present still, but they are complemented by gentleness and adaptability.

This Danish import, like all English and most European Great Danes has natural, uncropped ears.

By late in the nineteenth century, and into the early twentieth century, there were several major breeders of Great Danes in Germany. Before the first World War they traveled from London to St. Petersburg with twenty or thirty dogs apiece for the great dog shows of the time. It is interesting to think about these men traveling with that many dogs—especially given the size of Great Danes—with the transportation available in those years. Entries of Danes in the Stuttgart, Belgium and other shows on the continent numbered 100-300 Great Danes per show and dogs were exported from Germany to Moscow (including a great foundation dog named Hannibal I). Many also went to England, the United States, France and the Netherlands.

World War I had a devastating effect on breeding programs of all types of dogs, but of the Great Dane in particular. Many of the big breeders lost their money. Dogs were killed during the war, and after the war, good breeding stock was hard to find. Many breeders found themselves using dogs with light eyes or poor structure which they would not have used before the war.

The breed had just begun to build back to some of its original quality when World War II presented the problems of food shortages and air raids and again devastated the breed. But this time the German breeders were determined to hold onto their dogs. As late into the war as 1941, the Stuttgart dog show was still held and fifty-one Great Danes competed. In spite of the hardships, the breed emerged from World War II in better condition than it had been at the end of World War I in 1918.

In the United States, in spite of the wars, the Westminister Kennel Club show at Madison Square Garden never missed a year. Great Danes have held somewhat steady in numbers throughout this century. The quality of the breed has cycled up with some of the well known

kennels breeding strong for a decade or so, and then becoming less active. During some of these times the quality of the breed has gone down until other strong dogs came out to bring the quality back up. In this way, many of our breeders believe the breed has remained at about the same level of popularity and quality throughout this century. Though other breeds have been indiscriminately bred in the last fifty years, the Great Dane has never suffered from the abuse of overbreeding. One reason is that the Great Dane is large and difficult to house during pregnancy and whelping, and very expensive to raise due to ear cropping and health issues.

One unfortunate way that the breed has changed is the shortening of the life span. Although some lines and some individual dogs do live to be ten years old or more, many dogs are not living more than six or seven years. One breeder, who began breeding Great Danes in 1954, writes that in those days, the life span was twelve to thirteen years. Another breeder writes that in the early 1970s the dogs lived to be nine or ten on an average. However, she also said that in those days the good size bitch was only thirty-two inches and that a thirty-seven inch male was considered VERY

Olympic Athlete Greg Louganis with his Champion Harlequin Great Dane

large. Today, bitches are often thirty-four or thirty-five inches, and males are often thirty-seven or thirty-eight inches tall at the shoulders.

According to one breeder, bloat, a serious problem which plagues not only Great Danes, but most large, deep chested breeds, was not seen in Danes until the early 1970s. Although both the Morris Animal Foundation and Cornell University have been researching the problem for many years, there has not been much headway. Many answers have been purported, but neither cause nor solution has been firmly proven. We will talk more about this problem in the chapter on health.

THE GREAT DANE AROUND THE WORLD

The Great Dane has developed steadily in popularity all over the world. Almost all national standards are based on the original German standard. France, Italy, India, England and Holland use almost exact translations of the German standard.

Until the 1970s, most of the Great Dane kennels around the world were based on German lines. Japan, for example, had been steadily importing dogs from Germany since World War II. By the last quarter of this century however, American breeders were becoming well recognized around the world. Today, many of the top winning dogs in Japan are heavily mixed with American bloodlines. The Japanese lines are an example of what has happened in many countries throughout the world. German and American lines have mixed to provide a uniformity of the breed. Some breeders in our Hall of Fame section (beginning on page 64), and others throughout the country, have imported dogs from Germany. The world of the Great Dane truly stretches around the globe.

SHOULD YOU BUY A GREAT DANE?

*T*he most impressive characteristic of a Great Dane is the size. He is magnificent, elegant, regal and very large. The sheer practicality of living with a dog whose back is nearly the height of a kitchen cabinet, and who will take up as much as three by four feet of floor space when stretched out (usually in a doorway or in the middle of the traffic pattern of any room!) can be a significant challenge. His tail will easily clear off a coffee table, including the porcelain statue or an ashtray full of cigarettes. Standing on all four feet, the head of the average Great Dane will be about chest height on the average adult. And when a Great Dane leans into you for a scratch on the head or a pat on the back, he may weigh as much as his owner.

Before buying a puppy or adult dog, consider if you are ready to buy a dog at all and make a few basic decisions. Dogs, unlike fish or plants, take a commitment of time, energy and money beyond the initial purchase and act of feeding and watering them. Great Danes especially take a commitment. They are expensive to buy, and although they do not eat any more than any other large breed, they do eat a lot more than a Poodle! Vet bills are expensive, first because of some of the health problems, and second because of their size. Spaying and neutering, for example, will probably cost more because many vets do not have tables to accommodate a Great Dane and must have extra assistants to help with the dog while it is under the anesthetic. Boarding and bathing are often charged by the size of the dog, and can be expensive if you travel frequently.

You will need to invest time in a pup to keep an eye on his growth, making sure he is developing properly. The Great Dane is not a buy-and-forget kind of breed. He is a companion dog and needs your time investment to become the kind of companion that will fit into your life. Dogs are not mail order items, arriving complete with a set of instructions and a predetermined personality. They are interactive; they are bred to have certain basic traits and sensitivities, but they will develop according to their environment and influences.

The Great Dane is adaptable He can be many things, seemingly contradictory, at the same time. The following poem by an unknown author describes the breed best:

> The Great Dane is a man's dog;
>   he is big, fast, powerful, and courageous.
> The Great Dane is a woman's dog;
>   he is gentle, affectionate, and protective.
> The Great Dane is a child's dog
>   with his inborn patience and understanding.

When you have made the decision to acquire a new dog, take your time and do your homework. If properly raised, this animal will be part of your life for many years to come. He will live with you, sleep in your home and perhaps even your bed. He will share your hopes and joys and sorrows. He will need care and attention on a daily basis, 365 days a year. Not every breed of dog is suitable for every family. Even if you are attracted to the looks or the size of the Great Dane, realize that living with him on a full time basis is not for everyone. Remember that not all breeds are alike, and temperaments will vary widely among them. Once

This fawn puppy's ears look way too large for him, but he will grow until they are in proportion to his body and elegant head.

you have decided on a breed which is attractive to you, has the temperament to fit into your home and seems able to fill the need you have for a dog, be it companionship, babysitting, competition, protection or field work, you will need to find an individual animal of that breed which has been bred for those purposes in order to be sure he will fit well into your home and family.

The Great Dane is a large, strong dog which combines grace, beauty and elegance with power and strength. A Great Dane is a wonderful companion. He is very intelligent, loving and faithful to the family. He is not a one-person dog, but will eagerly share his affections with a wide variety of people. And he will change families easily, even as an adult. One breeder says that she has placed adult dogs and had them return for a visit with their new owners as little as a month or two later. They were happy to see her, they played and were at ease, but they were happy to say good-bye and get into the car, driving out of the driveway with their new owners as contented and at ease as they had ever been in their original home.

For that reason, if you are considering a new dog but a puppy does not seem to fit into your lifestyle, you might consider an adult. People with work schedules which do not allow them to come home in the middle of the day to care for a pup, people who do not have the time to socialize a puppy or do not care to go through the digging, chewing and general mischief stages and those who want to travel with their dog from the beginning will be well served with an adult dog. Many times a breeder will keep a likely show prospect, hoping he will be the world beater they have been looking for. (Every breeder is looking for that big winner.) Or, they may have kept two littermates to see which one will turn out better. Sometimes they have a dog they have taken back for one reason or another. There are many different reasons why a breeder may have a VERY nice quality, well-mannered dog which needs a good home. These dogs are gener-

ally well socialized; often they have been show dogs and are accustomed to traveling and the noise and confusion of a show. They are leash trained, at ease around strangers, and adaptable. They make excellent pets and should be considered. A puppy is cute, but he will grow up to be a very large dog. An adult dog gives you the advantage of seeing just how large your dog will be, and whether he fits into the back seat of the car! Keep in mind Great Danes are very slow to mature. They will take eighteen months to two years to settle 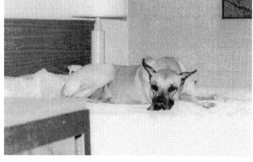 down and to be quiet and reliable. In the meantime, they may chew and dig and sometimes they play wonderful tricks like running the toilet paper through the house or pulling all the Kleenex out of the box. If you or your home and family are not ready to accommodate puppy behavior, you might want to think about an older dog.

Most adult Great Danes can be real couch potatoes. Even in country living on large estates, they may be under-exercised. If you don't exercise them, they will often be content to lie in the sun and snooze ("sunshine aerobics," as one of our breeders put it). For that reason, many breeders say Danes do just fine in small houses, or even townhouses or apartments if someone takes the time to exercise them properly. Unlike Labradors or Dobermans, for example, these dogs do not like to simply run and run for the joy of doing it.

They will play and roughhouse with each other, using their feet, mouths and bodies to slam and bat each other. They also will play with other breeds though this form of play can be very hard on a small dog. But Great Danes are most happy to play with a human. Some of our breeders report that they play with a stick or a ball, but others said the Great Dane is happier playing tag or hide-and-seek with the human(s) in his life. They are very quick to grasp the rules of these games and can play for hours. This interaction is a better alternative to, say, tug of war, which may cause damage to the teeth or bite, especially on a young pup, and sometimes has little appeal for the dog. Additionally, the dog's size advantage makes a game of tug of war almost an inevitable win for the full-grown Dane. They often will play with humans the same way they play with other dogs, slamming their bodies into people, using their feet and mouths, and generally overpowering even an adult human. For this reason, as we will say throughout this book, it is important to establish patterns of acceptable behavior, including play patterns, when the pup is small. Don't let a puppy play rough if you are not going to want the full-grown dog to play rough.

Most of them like to "mouth." That is, they will take your arm, leg or hand in their mouth. Though they do this gently, it is a part of their personality which may take some getting used to. Some breeders suggest that this springs from the behavior of pulling down the boar during a hunt, while other breeders disagree, because there is no aggressive behavior connected with it. It is more like a caress or a hug. Again, decide early if this is a behavior you can live with in a full-grown Great Dane and, if not, take steps to eliminate it early in the pup's life.

Advantages of a Great Danes include the fact that they are generally not aggressive, either to people or to other dogs. They are good watch dogs because of their size and deep bark, but generally their guarding instincts involve a wait-and-see attitude before they attack. This hesitancy is fortunate because a dog the size of a Great Dane, ready to attack, could easily be a lethal weapon. Although slow to take action, they will sound the alarm and take a stand, which is usually sufficient to deter any problem. A breeder tells about the time the house next door to hers was burglarized in the middle of the afternoon. The neighboring house had a burglar alarm which was bypassed. At the time she was gone, and her house was unlocked, but there was a brindle Great Dane bitch standing in the window barking. The burglars had preferred taking their chances with the alarm.

Early ear care is very important. Find someone near you or ask your breeder for help if you are not familiar with the process of getting ears to stand.

Great Danes are not overly "busy" dogs, at least not once they are full-grown. This is another reason why they make good house dogs. They are content to lie in the same room with the owner as the family goes about its daily activity. However, most breeders say they are apt to lie in the middle of the traffic pattern, often making chores and activities flow around them. Rather than chew up a toy, once they are adults, they will often carry around a favorite toy, keeping it in good condition for years. Sometimes they will take this to such extremes that they will carry around the toy for hours at a time, and can rarely be seen without it. One breeder says she capitalized on the trait by teaching her dogs to carry baskets from room to room as she did chores around the house and had even trained them to carry written messages from person to person throughout the house. Other dogs have completely outgrown toys of any kind by the time they are two years old.

Great Danes generally have very good eyesight and more than one has been reported watching TV, paying attention to other dogs and cats which may run across the screen from time to time.

Most Great Danes are fairly placid. They prefer to take life as it comes and do not become nervous or upset about most things. This outlook on life comes naturally with solid, consistent puppy raising and good socialization and does not require excessive effort on the part of the owner, besides providing a good, stable environment mixed with love and companionship. But remember that pups do make mistakes; they have accidents and throw up on the floor occasionally. If you cannot tolerate this and take it as part of raising a pup, don't get a Great Dane (or any other puppy for that matter), as you will raise a nervous, unstable dog and a Great Dane is far too large for that.

Another advantage of Great Danes is that they are affectionate without being clingy or fawning. They are lovely to look at and low in maintenance. They do what you are interested in and are adaptable. Families who enjoy boating, for example, have Danes who love the water, while other Danes would not get near water if you enticed them with a steak. Families with children have Danes who love kids and older couples who are not very active have Danes who are real couch potatoes.

Great Danes are usually outgoing, friendly and are reasonably stable. The reason we qualify these attributes with the words "usually" and "reasonably" is that the Great Dane is so adaptable that if he is raised in a household where the people are flighty, nervous, or otherwise unstable, the dog is very likely to be the same way. They adapt to their environment, reflecting it, both good and bad.

Most Great Danes excel in public relations. They enjoy crowds and meeting strangers, and enthusiastically enjoy praise and pats. Their quiet nature and love of new people and activities make them great therapy dogs in spite of their size.

One of the disadvantages of Great Danes is that they are somewhat delicate. Many need to have their diet changed gradually if a change becomes necessary. Although some can eat table scraps, many breeders say table scraps are not a good idea. First, they upset the balance of nutritional dog food. Second, because table scraps often do not agree with the dog's system, causing digestive problems. Finally, the Great Dane is often a picky eater. When fed table scraps, they will often learn to simply wait for something more tasty than dog food, making it even harder to keep weight on them.

Other disadvantages are bone and growth problems. Although these will be discussed in more detail in the health chapter, it is sufficient to say here that the Great Dane must be care-fully watched and monitored during his growth period for a wide variety of problems. This may be another reason to get an older dog. Hand in hand with these problems is a short life-span.

Finally, there is the disadvantage of living with a dog of that size. He does not fit well in many homes, and travel may be difficult or impractical as a Dane is too large to fit in a standard airline crate and takes up the entire back seat of a car.

Just being around something which takes up that much space in the house, your car and your life takes some getting used to. If you let the dog sit or sleep on the furniture, the chair or sofa will likely begin to sag under the weight in a few years. They even may sit on a chair with their rear end only, leaving their front feet on the floor since their entire body does not fit on the chair.

Although they are fairly easy to train, and do not need to be dominated as do some more aggressive breeds, their size alone makes it necessary to do early training. A dog which does not walk on a leash or does not

In spite of their size, their natural, good disposition make Great Danes wonderful therapy dogs, or participants in various other community visitation programs. Pictured here are two Danes enjoying a visit to the local elementary school. This gives students who may not own a dog or who have never seen a dog as large as a Great Dane a chance to gain confidence and an appreciation of pet ownership.

have any manners but which weighs only ten pounds is very different from a full-grown Great Dane which pulls on a leash, must be dragged into the veterinary office, or leaps up to say hello every time you come home. Remember, this is a dog which is large enough to eat off a plate sitting on the counter or the table without stretching at all. Make sure he has manners from the very beginning. You will need to have a fenced yard so he does not become a nuisance in the neighborhood. Although you may love your large dog and know how loving he is, you may find neighbors who have negative reactions to the size alone. Be sure he is kept on your property and has manners enough to maintain friendly neighborhood relations on the occasions he is out with family members.

Danes are gentle giants, but they are fairly fragile. Nothing annoys breeders more than someone talking about letting the kids ride the dog. Great Danes are not especially strong orthopedically. A dog is not designed to carry weight on his back like a horse or a mule. To set even a small child on the back of a Great Dane and expect him to carry the child around is to ask for physical problems which can be an annoyance to a dog at best and cruel at worst. Please do not annoy breeders and owners of Great Danes by making such comments.

At one time, Harlequins (see the chapter on color) were said to be larger in bone, coarser in build, harder headed and more difficult to handle than other colors. Blacks were sometimes thought to be lighter and perhaps a little more nervous. This does not seem to be the case anymore. Careful breeding for temperament and structure has evened out the differences. One difference you will find is the price. Because Harlequins are so hard to breed, they are higher in price than the other colors, though *mismarked* Harlequins may be less expensive than other colors. A good Harlequin may also be more difficult to find.

Expect to pay $500 to $700 for a Fawn, Black or Brindle, and $800 or more for a Harlequin or Blue. These prices will vary from breeder to breeder, but they generally go up, not down from this point. Males may cost more than females simply because of demand. Since size is important to many buyers of the breed, and most males are larger than females, many breeders said they had more requests for male pups than female. A female makes just as good a pet as does a male and should be considered. Once a dog is thirty-four or more inches tall, does another inch or two make a real difference? Some of our breeders felt males tend to be more affectionate and clinging, while females are better for obedience work because they tend to be more serious and precise. If you have several males, it is harder to keep order and be sure there are no fights. If you have just two dogs, a male and a female make the best combination. However, unspayed females will frequently go through false pregnancies. During this time they dig, both in the garden and even at carpet, in an instinct to "bed" or "nest." Since pets should always be spayed or neutered, this should not be a concern as false pregnancies do not occur once a bitch is spayed.

What do you want the dog to do? Will he be a companion who travels with you? If you travel frequently, how will you provide care for him while you are gone? Do you want him to amuse himself until you call him, or do you want him to remind you that it is time to take a few minutes to pay attention to him? Who will take care of the dog on a daily basis? Will there be children who come in on a regular basis or do you have children — or are you planning a family in the future? Does everyone in the family want a dog — this dog in particular? What kind of personality do you and other members of the family have and what kinds of people or animals do you work well with? Is this dog expected to be friendly toward strangers or primarily a guard dog? Some of these answers will point you toward a Great Dane, and others will not.

Evaluate your home. How much room do you have for a dog? Do you have a fenced yard? Do you have time for a dog? Are there other pets in the family? Great Danes usually get along well with other animals, but how will the other animals feel about the new addition?

Once you have decided that you are ready for a dog and have read this book, and if you are still considering a Great Dane, talk to several breeders. Ask about factors which are important to you in your situation. Each year, hundreds and thousands of lovely, purebred dogs end up at the SPCA, and people who have invested money in a good dog are discouraged to find that the pet they dreamed would become a part of their lives for years to come has become a nightmare. Not *every* dog in the breed will be the same and not *every* home is the same. What will fit one family will be a disaster in another. People have different life patterns and different lifestyles, not to mention differences in homes, yards and time commitments. And people are attracted to different personalities in dogs. What may be fun and appealing to one person may be tiresome and destructive to another. It is important that you begin the process of looking for a dog by carefully evaluating what you want the dog to do, how you want it to behave, and how you want it to live.

Most dogs end up in the SPCA not because they are *bad* dogs, but because they did not fit their homes. Think about it as if you wanted a sports car, but had five children to carry around! Before long, the sports car would be up for sale, not because sports cars are not good cars, but because it did not perform well in the given situation. The car simply could not do the job the family with five children needed it to do. It did not fit the situation or the home of the driver. The same is true with dogs. If the dog does not fit your home and lifestyle, no matter how appealing you find the breed, it will not be long before the needs of the dog and the needs of the family are in conflict.

Within each breed, there will be conflicting views of the breed among breeders (we will discuss this more in the chapter on finding a breeder). Most breeders will tell you that their breed is the best. If they didn't think so, they would be putting their time and energy into a different breed. Sometimes dog breeders raise or show several breeds before settling on the one to which they will dedicate their lives and fortunes!

Different breeds have the *tendency* toward certain characteristics based on their history, temperament, size and physical limitations or attributes. Talking with individual breeders will give you an idea of how different breeders see the breed. Also, it is important to realize that not all dogs within the same breed are alike. Not only are there differences between individual dogs, even within the same litter, but within the breed there are differences in "style," which simply means the ways in which individual dogs within the breed differ from each other. Again, talking with individual breeders will allow you to decide what "style" is right for you.

If you purchase a puppy, will you have him cropped and do you have time to do the ear care for the next three or four months? An older dog may be cropped already, but if it is not, you will not be able to get the ears to stand even if you have them cropped. What the ears look like on an older dog is what they will look like for the rest of his life.

An uncropped Great Dane has a completely different look. Pet owners may opt for uncropped ears for a variety of reasons. Most Danes are compatible with other breeds such as this Saint Bernard.

A puppy may have his ears cropped already. Many breeders feel that the standing ear is part of what gives the Great Dane the look of elegance so much a part of the breed. Other breeders are not fond of cropping and may leave pet pups uncropped. As we have mentioned, cropped ears are not a part of the breed in Great Britain, and there are movements within this country to either eliminate cropping or at least make uncropped dogs more acceptable to the general public. If you do not want a dog with cropped ears, we suggest you either buy a very young puppy, or find a breeder who does not crop the ears on his pets. Because feelings sometimes run high on this subject, we suggest you

This lovely fawn thinks he is a couch dog in spite of his size. Just living with a dog the size of a Great Dane is something a prospective owner needs to think about. Right from the beginning you need to decide if you will allow the dog on the furniture and not count on the fact that once he is full grown he will naturally stop because he is too big!

approach the subject carefully, asking the breeder how he feels about ear cropping on pets before you interject your feelings.

Ear cropping will run anywhere from $80 or $100 per dog if the litter is done all at one time by the breeder, and may be as high as $150 or $200 if an individual dog is done by your vet. You will need to find a vet who knows about ear cropping and is willing to do it. (Some vets do not like the practice and refuse to do it.) You will pay for it one way or the other, either in direct charges to the vet or in a higher purchase price from the breeder. Dogs need to be cropped between seven and fourteen weeks, but eight weeks is generally considered the ideal time. The older the pup, the more likely the ears will not stand properly. The style of the crop is also important as long, thin crops are harder to make stand than shorter, wider crops. Look in the Hall of Fame to see the different crops and ear styles even among famous dogs. (See the chapter on care for more about ear cropping.)

In England, where cropping has not been legal for almost one hundred years, Danes are bred to have small, attractive ears mounted high on their heads such as the Danish dog on page 11. Compare this dog's ears, which go up and then break over, to other uncropped ears in this book to see the difference. Because ears are usually cropped in the United States, breeders select for large ears which will give plenty of excess leather to get the correct crop. Ears are thick and heavy with strong muscling to give erectile power. This means that if left uncropped, the ears will be large and somewhat clumsy looking.

THE STANDARD

*T*he Standard is very important to breeders because it gives them something written against which to measure their dogs. Unlike dog shows, where the judge bases his decision on what is the best dog being presented to him from those entries which are showing that day, the Standard describes the ideal dog of any breed. Without a written Standard describing what the breed should look like, a breed would change freely at the whim of what was popular with judges and breeders at the time. In a few generations the breed would look completely different. The Standard pulls the breed back to the middle of the range, but individual dogs will vary in some ways. In fact, there is seldom, if ever, a dog which meets the Standard perfectly. Breeding with the Standard in mind is one thing that marks the difference between "Good Breeders" and "Puppy Mills," or uneducated "Backyard Breeders." Breeders who take the time and trouble to learn their breed, to evaluate their dogs, and to make informed breedings which will keep their puppies in the range where they are still easily recognizable as their breed are those who best ensure the future of the Great Dane.

In general, a Great Dane should be elegant, not dainty. In the past, Danes where often crossed between mastiffs and greyhounds, but today should not be mistaken for either breed.

Many times pet owners will ask why it is important to them if the breeder breeds to the Standard. The reason is quite obvious. If, as a new owner, you have taken the time to look into the breed, to select one which fits your family and your needs, and one whose appearance is pleasing to you, and you purchase a puppy based on that decision, you have the right to a dog which will grow up and be recognizable as that breed. As long as a dog has AKC papers, and it is bred to a bitch with AKC papers, and the paperwork is in order, AKC will issue papers for puppies. But that does not ensure that those puppies will indeed grow up to be representative of their breed. For that, you must trust your breeder and his knowledge of the breed Standard.

Every breed which shows anywhere in the world has a written Standard of the Breed by which the dog is judged. The Standard may vary from country to country, in details, though it is generally very similar, since it describes the same breed no matter what the country. This Standard is important in preserving "breed type,"

in layman's terms, those characteristics which make a Great Dane a Great Dane and not a Rottweiler! The American Standard of the Great Dane has always been based on the German Standard, as adopted by the Deutsche Doggen Club. In fact, all nations have recognized the authority of Germany in this matter. The American Standard is written by the breed club in this country, and was revised in 1944, 1976 and 1990. The last modification was part of an effort by AKC to get breed Standards for all breeds to fit a consistent format. For many years, the Great Dane Standard used in this country was one of the longest breed Standards in AKC. It included a scale of points for each part of the dog. The total was 100, and, for example, the general appearance was worth ten points, the head, twelve points, teeth, four points and so on. It also cited a Porcelain Statue by Rosenthal ("Deutsche Dogge" No. 960-1, 2046-1) as the ideal conformation of an ideal Great Dane. Today the Standard does not include a point scale.

"Style" is how the individual dog looks. Although the dog is easy to recognize as a Great Dane, for example, and he fits the Standard, there are always words and phrases which are subject to interpretation. Breeders and judges may disagree on exactly what the Standard means by placing different emphasis on different words and phrases. This variance leads to slight differences in the look of the individual dog from country to country, from one geographic location to another within the United States, and even between kennels. We suggest you take a good look at the "Hall of Fame" section. Look at the different dogs and try to see the difference in looks, or "style," between them. Then look at the pedigrees beneath the pictures. Are there similar names in the pedigrees of the dogs you like? See if you can identify why some of the dogs will be more appealing to you than others. All of the dogs pictured in the Hall of Fame are outstanding dogs of their breed. They have earned the right to be in this section. But because of the difference in interpretation of the breed Standard, and the different purposes for which the breeder wishes his dogs to be used, there will be differences between dogs in what is referred to as "style."

The Standard for Great Danes reads as follows:

GENERAL APPEARANCE — The Great Dane combines, in its regal appearance, dignity, strength and elegance with great size and a powerful, well-formed, smoothly muscled body. It is one of the giant working breeds, but is unique in that its general conformation must be so well-balanced that it never appears clumsy, and shall move with a long reach and powerful drive. It is always a unit — the Apollo of dogs. A Great Dane must be spirited, courageous, never timid; always friendly and dependable. This physical and mental combination is the characteristic which gives the Great Dane the majesty possessed by no other breed. It is particularly true of this breed that there is an impression of great masculinity in dogs, as compared to an impression of femininity in bitches. Lack of true Dane breed type, as defined in this Standard, is a serious fault.

SIZE, PROPORTION, SUBSTANCE — The male should appear more massive throughout than the bitch, with larger frame and heavier bone. In the ratio between length and height, the Great Dane should be square. In bitches, a somewhat longer body is permissible, providing she is well-proportioned to her height. Coarseness or lack of substance are equally undesirable. The male shall not be less than 30 inches at shoulders, but it is preferable that he be 32 inches or more, providing he is well-proportioned to his height. The female shall not be less than 28 inches at shoulders, but it is preferable that she be 30 inches or more, providing she is well-proportioned to her height. Danes under minimum height must be disqualified.

HEAD — The head shall be rectangular, long, distinguished, expressive, finely chiseled, especially below the eyes. Seen from the side, the Dane's forehead must be sharply set off from the bridge of the nose (a strongly pronounced stop). The plane of the skull and the plane of the muzzle must be straight and parallel to one another. The skull plane under and to the inner point of the eye must slope without any bony protuberance in a smooth line to a full square jaw with deep muzzle (fluttering lips are undesirable). The masculinity of the male is very pronounced in structural appearance of the head. The bitch's head is more delicately formed. Seen from the top, the skull should have parallel sides and the bridge of the nose should be as broad as possible. The cheek muscles should not be prominent. The length from the tip of the nose to the center of the stop should be equal to the length from the center of the stop to the rear of the slightly developed occiput. The head should be angular from all sides and should have flat planes with dimensions in proportion to the size of the Dane. Whiskers may be trimmed or left natural. **Eyes** — Shall be medium-size, deep-set and dark, with a lively intelligent expression. The eyelids are almond-shaped and relatively tight, with well-developed brows.   Haws and Mongolian eyes are serious faults.   In harlequins, the eyes should be dark; light-colored eyes, eyes of different colors and walleyes are permitted but not desirable.   **Ears** — Shall be high-set, medium in size and of moderate thickness, folded forward close to the cheek.   The topline of the folded ear should be level with the skull.   If cropped, the ear length is in proportion to the size of the head and the ears are carried uniformly erect.   **Nose** — Shall be black, except in the blue Dane, where it is a dark blue-black.   A black spotted nose is permitted on the harlequin; a pink-colored nose is not desirable.   A split nose is a disqualification.   **Teeth** — Shall be strong, well-developed, clean and with full dentition.   The incisors of the lower jaw touch very lightly the bottoms of the inner surface of the upper incisors (scissors bite).   An undershot jaw is a very serious fault.   Overshot or wry bites are serious faults.   Even bites, misaligned or crowded incisors are minor faults.

NECK, TOPLINE, BODY — The neck shall be firm, high-set, well-arched, long and muscular. From the nape, it should gradually broaden and flow smoothly into the withers.   The neck underline should be clean.   Withers shall slope smoothly into a short, level back with a broad loin.   The chest shall be broad, deep and well-muscled.   The forechest should be well-developed without a pronounced sternum.   The brisket extends to the elbow, with well-sprung ribs.   The body underline should be tightly muscled with a well-defined tuck-up.   The croup should be broad and very slightly sloping.   The tail should be set high and smoothly into the croup, but not quite level with the back, a continuation of the spine.   The tail should be broad at the base, tapering uniformly down to the hock joint.   At rest, the tail should fall straight.   When excited or running, it may curve slightly, but never above the level of the back.   A ring or hooked tail is a serious fault.   A docked tail is a disqualification.

FOREQUARTERS — The forequarters, viewed from the side, shall be strong and muscular. The shoulder blade must be strong and sloping, forming, as near as possible, a right angle in its articulation with the upper arm.   A line from the upper tip of the shoulder to the back of the elbow joint should be perpendicular.   The ligaments and muscles holding the shoulder blade to the rib cage must be well-developed, firm and securely attached to prevent loose shoulders. The shoulder blade and the upper arm should be the same length.   The elbow should be one-half the distance from the withers to the ground.   The strong pasterns should slope slightly. The feet should be round and compact with well-arched toes, neither toeing in, toeing out nor rolling to the inside or outside.   The nails should be short, strong and as dark as possible, except that they may be lighter in harlequins.   Dewclaws may or may not be removed.

HINDQUARTERS — Hindquarters shall be strong, broad, muscular and well-angulated, with well-let-down hocks.   Seen from the rear, the hock joints appear to be perfectly straight, turned neither toward the inside nor toward the outside.   Rear feet should be round and compact, with well-arched toes, neither toeing in nor out.   The nails should be short, strong and as dark as possible, except they may be lighter in harlequins.   Wolf claws are a serious fault.

COAT — The coat shall be short, thick and clean with a smooth, glossy appearance.

COLOR, MARKINGS AND PATTERNS — **Brindle** — Base color shall be yellow gold and always brindled with strong black cross stripes in a chevron pattern.   A black mask is preferred.   Black should appear on the eye rims and eyebrows, and may appear on ears and tail tip.   The more intensive the base color and the more distinct and even the brindeling, the more preferred will be the color.   Too much or too little brindeling are equally undesirable. White markings at the chest and toes, black-fronted, dirty-colored brindles are not desirable. **Fawn** — Color shall be yellow gold with a black mask.   Black should appear on the eye rims and eyebrows, and may appear on the ears and tail tip.   The deep yellow gold must always be given the preference.   White markings at the chest and toes, black-fronted, dirty-colored fawns are not desirable.   **Blue** — color shall be a pure steel blue.   White markings at the chest and toes are not desirable.   **Black** — Color shall be a glossy black.   White markings at the chest and toes are not desirable.   **Harlequin** — Base color shall be pure white with black torn patches irregularly and well-distributed over the entire body; a pure white neck is preferred.   The black patches should never be large enough to give the appearance of a blanket, nor so small as to give a stippled or dappled effect.   Eligible, but less desirable, are a few small gray patches, or a white base with single black hairs showing through, which tend to give a salt-and-pepper or dirty effect.   Any variance in color or markings as described above shall be faulted to the extent of the deviation.   Any Great Dane which does not fall within the above color classifications must be disqualified.

GAIT — Denotes strength and power with long, easy strides resulting in no tossing, rolling or bouncing of the topline or body. Backline shall appear level and parallel to the ground. The long reach should strike the ground below the nose while the head is carried forward. The powerful rear drive should be balanced to the reach. As speed increases, there is a natural tendency for the legs to converge toward the center line of balance beneath the body. There should be no twisting in or out at the elbow or hock joints.

TEMPERAMENT — The Great Dane must be spirited, courageous, always friendly and dependable, and never timid or aggressive.

DISQUALIFICATIONS — Danes under minimum height. Split nose. Docked tail. Any color other than those described under "Color, Markings and Patterns."

All of this is a very complex way of describing what a Great Dane should look like, and why it does not look like any other breed. Some of the terms used are historical, such as the description of the expression as being "the Apollo of dogs." Other terms are specific for dog show judging, or are widely accepted terms in judging animals. When the Standard refers to "well-let-down hocks," all judges and breeders understand what that means regardless of the breed described. Other terms refer to specific parts of the dog such as "a strongly pronounced stop." This description of the head means that there is a sharp drop between the flat top part of the head behind the eye and the flat part of the muzzle between the eyes and the nose. "Withers" and "croup" are terms which describe body parts of most animals, from dogs and horses to sheep and cattle. The withers are the shoulders; the croup is the area from the hip to the tail.

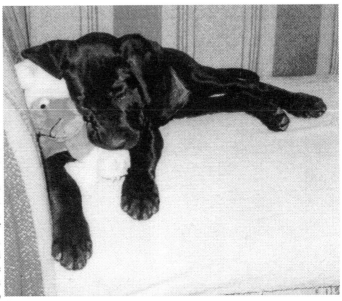

In layman's terms, this Standard describes a dog whose back will be about hip high on the average adult. The Great Dane should be elegant and graceful looking, instead of stocky like a Rottweiler. The Great Dane is about as tall as it is long (measuring from the ground to the back and from the chest to the rear of the dog and does not include the head, neck or tail). It has strong bones, a broad head that resembles a rectangular box for the muzzle, connected to a square box which is the skull. The muzzle should NOT come to a point. The back is level — straight without lumps, dips or slants — and the tail is long. The dog may have either cropped or uncropped ears, though in this country, cropped ears are more common. The dog should not be clumsy looking, nor skinny and delicate looking. It should move with a powerful, easy gait, covering the ground in long strides.

It is important to know the Standard is not something you will need to study if you have simply bought a nice pet from a good breeder. Your dog, because of his genetic heritage, will look like his breed, and his breeder will be able to tell you exactly where he deviates from the Standard, and what makes him a pet. If you buy a dog from someone who does NOT know the Standard, however, the chances are that the breeding has not been done with the ideal dog in mind, and the puppy produced may not look anything like the dog we have described above, or what you have in mind when you picture a Great Dane. Before you consider breeding your dog, you will need to learn the Standard, learn how it applies to dogs and your dog in particular and learn how to evaluate the strengths and weaknesses in your bitch or dog. You should seek out a mate which will be strong where your animal is weak, thus pulling the puppies back toward the Standard for the breed.

When you talk to a breeder, he should be able to tell you about the Standard and how his dogs compare. Remember, there is no dog which perfectly matches the Standard, but it is important for a breeder to know his dogs well.

"Style" is another thing which will affect a breeding or a kennel. Some terms in the Standard are very specific and do not allow for any interpretation. The size is stated in terms of inches, and is easy to measure. But one breeder may have an outstanding dog which is either above or below the size stated in the Standard, and may still use him for breeding because he may have an outstanding head and good proportion, and be an excellent mover with strong hips. Another breeder may see the same dog, focus on the size, and refuse to use him for breeding because in that one respect, he does not meet the exact size requirements of the Standard. This is because some breeders will look at the overall dog, and if it is particularly nice or has a look which that breeder feels is especially good for the breed, they will use the dog for breeding even if it has a specific fault. Other breeders focus on the fault, and will use a dog which is not quite as nice over all but which does not have any specific faults. (We will discuss this more in the chapter on showing.)

One factor affecting this choice is if the breeder feels his dogs are weak in one area and the dog with the fault is especially strong in that area. Thus, a breeder who feels his bitch is too straight in the rear legs may breed to a dog that has weak color or a large white spot, but excellent angulation, especially if his bitch has good, strong color. He will hope that at least some of the puppies will have good color with the sire's angulation in the rear, and he will accept that some of the puppies

will not have the strong color or will have too much white on the chest to be good show dogs. These puppies will be pets. *No litter is all show dogs, no breeder produces all show dogs, and no kennel has dogs which all meet the Standard perfectly.* The joy and sport of breeding show dogs is the art of how close breeders can come to the Standard, and how often.

Other terms, such as "well-developed," "relatively tight" and "very slightly sloping" leave room for differences in opinion for each breeder to decide just how much he or she will or will not accept.

Finally, style is affected by what part of the dog each breeder feels is most important. Some breeders select their stock based on a good head or neck. Some will place primary importance on movement. Debate runs high between breeders who feel that different qualities are of primary importance for the breed. When you look at the Hall of Fame, you will see differences between the dogs. When you look at the pedigrees, then look back at the Standard, you have taken your first lesson in what the sport of dog breeding involves, and why it produces dogs with certain common characteristics. This will explain why some breeders will get $500 for a puppy, while others will advertise in the newspaper and ask only $200, and still others will get $1,500. For $3 more a month over the lifetime of the dog, one puppy will give you pride and joy and will have the characteristics people have come to associate with the breed, and one may be only a poor imitation. It is no wonder that most reputable breeders have no trouble selling their puppies, while inferior or poorly bred litters of puppies may be in the paper week after week still looking for homes.

FINDING A BREEDER

*B*efore you buy a dog, do your homework. Look into the breed and be sure it is one which will fit your family. Do your homework about breeds. Don't simply select a breed because you like the looks of it, or because Aunt Jennifer has one and you think it is fun to play with on the two times a year you visit. If you have the time, go to a local dog show. At the end of the day, the groups will have the best examples of each breed competing for the group placements and eventually Best in Show. This will give you a chance to see different breeds, maybe some you have never even considered. Sometimes the announcer will even give a commentary about the breed as it is showing in the group ring. Consider everything about a breed, including exercise, grooming and temperament. Evaluate your home situation and decide what place you want the dog to fill in your home.

Do you want the dog for showing, obedience, protection or companionship? Should it play with the children, be a traveling companion or jogging partner? Will someone be home all the time? Do you want a wonderful, appreciative warm being to come home to — one which will greet you at the door and unfailingly be happy to see you? Do you live alone or have a large family? Are there a lot of strangers in and out of the house?

Decide who will feed the dog, who will take care of the training and who will clean up after the dog. Especially if you have a puppy, there will be messes and accidents, trash pulled over and things chewed up. Are you prepared for those things? Do you accept the difference between wanting a well behaved dog and doing the training it takes to raise one? Will you be mad and frustrated when a problem, accident or mess occurs?

When you buy a dog, you are not just buying a television which will sit on your shelf quietly if you do not want to pay attention to it. You are buying a friend, a companion, a family member. Do it wisely. Educate yourself about the breed, and about breeders. You will live with this dog, he will share your life, your hopes and sorrows for seven years or more. As one breeder says, "For many people these days, the dog will outlast the marriage!" Take your time, choose well and buy from a careful, reputable breeder.

With all of these decisions firmly in mind, it is time to find a breeder and ask further questions. Find out what the breed is like from talking to several breeders, but be sure that you have intelligent questions before you begin. You will get much more appreciation and respect from breeders if you have taken the time to look into the breed before you call.

Technically, anyone who breeds an AKC registered litter is a breeder. There are so many kinds of breeders that it is easy to become confused. Some are focused on producing winning conformation Danes and breeding champions; some are focused on producing Danes with exceptional temperaments. Soundness and good structure may be the focus of other breeders. Finally there are profit oriented, business minded people, whose dogs range in quality from those of kennels operated by knowledgeable breeders who take good care of their animals to puppy mills where the health and welfare of the breeding stock is not an important consideration.

There are "backyard" breeders, who may be the worst kind. Their dogs are generally found in the newspaper, for cheap prices. The puppies may have been produced by someone who has a bitch they probably bought as a pet, then bred to the closest male they could find. They know nothing of the breed, what it should look like, health problems or temperament. They are starting with low quality and moving downhill! Spending even $200 for a pup from such a breeding is an invitation to disaster. It may not have the qualities you want in a dog when you selected the Great Dane as the breed for you. It may well grow up to be undersized, with health or temperament problems that the breeder has no idea how to correct, and be hard to identify as a Great Dane at all.

Think of a reputable breeder as a service oriented broker more than a discount retailer. He has taken the time and energy to be well educated and produce the best possible product he can, improving that product with each generation. He will take the time to get to know you, your family and what you need in a dog, and to know his pups on an individual basis. Finally, after you buy the pup, he will continue to help you with problems and advice until the pup is full-grown, and even throughout its life.

"Puppy mill" is another term you may hear. A puppy mill is a kennel which generally produces a large number of dogs, without regard for the breed or how the sire and dam match in pedigree, style, temperament or health. Their only goal is to cut corners where they can and produce pups which can be sold at the highest possible price. They have the same problems as the backyard breeder, but instead of doing it through ignorance, they do it for profit. Often these puppies make their way into pet shops, which sell them as impulse items to unwitting buyers. These pups may be poor in health, and often do not have the qualities for which the breed is known. This awareness of responsibility and sense of continuity makes the difference between a "reputable breeder" and a "puppy raiser." Most breeders see themselves as artists, and they are motivated by a drive to produce something perfect. Further, many see themselves as social workers, matching adoptive "children" to homes where they will be happy and where they will bring joy.

Not all breeders will agree on what defines perfection. Throughout the development of this book we found breeders who thought one dog was a wonderful example of the breed, and equally qualified breeders who thought that particular dog was not nearly as good as his win record would indicate.

The Standard is a written document, a blueprint, but each breeder will put emphasis on different parts of the dog, different words and different combinations of traits. Just as the same movie script could be shot by several different directors and produce several different films, all containing the same dialogue, but quite individual in many respects, so breeders, all dedicated to their breed, will produce dogs with different styles and types. It is through the combination of these efforts that the breed develops, yet remains consistent from generation to generation. It is the dedication to that effort that marks the responsible breeder.

A puppy raiser, puppy mill or backyard breeder has no such sense of history, dedication or creativity. Their only goal is to produce a product and sell it to the first available buyer for the agreed-upon price. The dogs are over-the-counter commodities. Such breeders do not see the link between the past and the future, and do not feel required to preserve that link. As a result, their choices of breedings (which stud is bred to which bitch) may be more a matter of convenience than of quality. The puppies they produce may be worse than the generation before, something which is a nightmare to good breeders who strive to make each generation better. It does not take a genius in genetics to realize that with an uncaring attitude, it only takes a few short generations before puppies advertised as "AKC registered Great Danes" may be that in name only. The AKC has no way to check the quality of the dogs registered, nor does it have the authority to refuse papers for any animal eligible for registration by virtue of the dog and bitch both being registered for breeding.

Even when buying a pet, you have a right to assume that the dog you buy will exhibit the traits characteristic of its breed. As we said in the introduction, if all you want is a warm animal to occupy your home, you can get a dog from the pound. But, just as with a car, if you want it to pull a trailer, you will not be happy with a Geo. A sports car will not be good for a family of five, and a person who admires quality and takes pride in what he drives as part of his image will not be happy with a used Hyundai.

A puppy raiser may be nothing more than a salesperson. A breeder asks questions, evaluates and educates. His goal is not simply to get the dog off of his food bill and the money into his pocket as soon as possible, and his job does not end with the sale and shipping. He will endeavor in his breeding program to produce the best possible example of the breed, and in his placement to ensure the best fit between the home and the puppy.

This does not mean that every puppy he produces will be a champion. In fact, beware of the breeder who tells you he produces nothing but show dogs. Every dog has some fault, and every litter has some "pets." But a reputable breeder should honestly and openly tell you why this dog is a pet and how well you can expect the dog to fit your home. The "pet" from a good litter will still be of much better quality than the best of a litter bred by a puppy mill or backyard breeder. It is like comparing the best player of a high school football team with a backup player in the NFL. The NFL player may not be the leader of his team, but he still has years of practice, hard work and the talent to have raised him to the standing which he enjoys, and he is still miles ahead of the high school player with little experience and an inflated idea of his own talent.

Luckily, find-ing a good breeder is not all that difficult. Going to a dog show is a good place to see Great Danes in action and begin your search. But don't expect to find puppies there. Good breeders — and AKC rules — keep pup-pies at home where they belong. Watch how the dogs react in the ring. Do they seem relaxed and happy or do they shy from the judge with a tucked tail? Buy a

show catalog which lists all of the entries and their sires and dams. See if the dogs you like are related. It is sometimes difficult to talk to breeders at a show because they may be busy getting their dogs ready for the ring. Most show people take these events very seriously and therefore may be short of small talk at the show. Remember these exhibitors have a lot invested in the show at hand in terms of entry fees, travel and perhaps handling expenses and advertising. Selling you a puppy or helping you to find one is not likely to be their first priority.

But, the show catalog will list, next to the name of each dog, the names of the breeder and owner. By watching the classes you can find dogs of the type and style you like and look up their owners. The address of the owner will be listed either with the entry, or in an index at the rear of the book. When you get home, call directory information for the number or write for information and a contact phone number.

Local kennel clubs may have a list of breeders in your area. Calling breeders included in some of the major dog publications is another way to begin finding a dog.

It is more important to find a breeder you are comfortable with than to find one close to your home. Going to visit a litter may be fun, but it may also lead to disaster. You may buy a dog you are not ready for just because the puppies are so cute. Or, the puppy which appeals to you may not be the best suited to your home situation. A good breeder, one who knows the bloodline and has watched the puppies from birth, will have a better idea of what will fit your lifestyle. Describe *how* you want the dog to fit into your household, what you expect it to do, and what your family is like. Ask the breeder how he or she feels on issues of importance to you. Listen carefully to the answers.

You need to know what the breeder will accept in his or her breeding stock, and what will cause him to reject a dog completely. These differences between breeders will, after generations, make the difference between dogs from different kennels. When you look through the Hall of Fame, read what the breeder has to say. See if his purpose in breeding matches your needs. Talk with breeders long enough to know where they place emphasis and what is not of  great importance to them, and see how it matches your view of the breed and what you want to use the dog for in your home. Then find a breeder with whom you agree and purchase a puppy from that person.

Most of our breeders agree that if you ask a breeder to name the most important factors in a dog or in his breeding program and he does not include health and temperament, you should probably look elsewhere if you are looking for a good pet. These are qualities you need just as much as you need a nice looking dog which is reflective of its breed. And these qualities are part of the reason we recommend buying from a reputable breeder.

In the end, you are often better off trusting the breeder to select a puppy for your family than in picking it yourself. You will see the puppies for only a short time. They may all look alike to you, especially if the entire litter is the same color. One may be tired after a morning of playing, it may have just eaten and be sleepy, or it may have just awakened or be reacting to a littermate in a way which is uncharacteristic. The breeder has seen this litter for weeks, watched them and compared them to other litters from the same bloodlines. He knows more about each puppy from his past experience than you can possibly see within the framework of a short visit. Remember, the selection you make will be with you for many years and should be based on sound judgment and as much information as possible before making a decision.

WHAT TO ASK A BREEDER

Be sure to identify the qualities you want in a dog. Have a list of questions and call several breeders. Ask them all the same questions and make notes of their answers. By comparing the similarities in the answers, you will see a picture emerge of what the breed is truly like, and how well it will fit your family. From the differences in the answers you will begin to find breeders who fit your needs and with whom you feel you can work comfortably.

Because temperament varies within the breed, between kennels, and between individuals, ask about how the breeder views the temperament of the breed in general, and this litter in particular. See how well the answers match your family and what you want in a pet. Inquire about socialization. How have the pups been raised and what kind of temperaments have been noticed? If you have children, see if the line is good with children, either in the home or in other homes where the bloodline has been sold. One of our breeders points out that if you are going to see the litter and the breeder asks that you leave your children at home, you should probably be very cautious and rethink the purchase.

Ask the breeder what health problems may be in the breed. If the breeder continually states that there are no problems in health or temperament, no problems in training, and generally represents the dog as nothing but a 100% ideal pet, be careful. Bloodlines have their good points and their bad points. A good breeder will know both the strengths and weaknesses. "Kennel blind" breeders (those who cannot see any faults in their own dogs — but are usually very good at seeing the faults in dogs from other kennels!) run the risk of overlooking faults and thereby breeding them into their dogs. A breeder cannot strive to eliminate a problem if he is too kennel blind to see it.

If you want a pet, ask *why* the dog is a pet then evaluate for yourself if the dog is a good buy. Many of the reasons for a dog to be classified as a pet are of no concern to the average pet owner. Unless you are used to critically evaluating dogs, you will not see a straight shoulder, or probably even a sagging topline. But if the dog is too light in bone and build to show, it will make a difference in the general appearance and may make it less appealing to you. If the eyes are too light, that fault will change the appearance and may make a difference to you. Beware of breeders who claim that this is a perfect dog which just happens to be selling in a pet price range. But realize that a good breeder knows the value of his dogs, and years of experience have taught him what a fair value is for the pups he produces, even those with faults. Don't ever argue about why this pup is not worth the money because the breeder has been honest enough to admit a fault!

A pet puppy will begin in a price range of $500 to $600, depending on the breeder and the puppy. Expect the price to go up with the quality of the puppy. An especially cute puppy may run $700 to $1,200. The breeder will price the puppy by how much he wants to keep the puppy for his own use as a breeding or show dog. When we talk about a bottom price, breeders take into consideration that some pups have faults. A big boned pup with a nice head and a lot of white, for example, may be priced at $500 because of his color. Don't assume that because there is a color fault the pups should be worth only $200! If this nice pup did not have the color fault he would be priced at $700 or more, depending on the kennel and the bloodline.

Likewise, if you want a good looking, top-quality dog with an attractive head, large, solid bones and a level topline, you may be looking for a show quality dog, even if it is simply for a pet. Do not expect a small price tag simply because you don't want to show. Remember that "pet" should be the function the dog will fill in your home, not necessarily the quality of the puppy. Often the same qualities which make a dog a good show dog, or working dog, also make it a fine example of the breed, and a quality dog is a quality dog whether or not it ever steps into the show ring. Remember, breeders price their puppies by the quality of the puppy, not by purpose of the buyer.

In Great Danes, one reason the price of pets remains high is that there is not as much indiscriminate breeding as there is in some breeds. Danes are expensive to raise and require a lot of space and immense time and care. Many breeders euthanize pups with obvious faults at birth in an effort to reduce the number of pups being

nursed by the dam. And, often the breeder wants to reduce the number of pet pups and pet owners he has to deal with. Our Hall of Fame breeders are willing to work with and educate new people, but it is up to you as a new buyer to try to ask good questions.

Like most of our breeders, one says she likes to stay in contact with her puppy buyers. (Many breeders actually refer to people who buy their pups as "my puppy people.") She says she tries to find people who are reasonable and easy to work with. She does not want to sell a puppy to someone who will call at midnight to say the puppy has just sneezed, but she does want buyers who will call when they have a question, need advice, or notice something that may be a problem. If they listen carefully and try to follow her advice, she can be sure that the new family and their dog are off to a good start.

CONTRACTS

Good breeders will give you a contract with your dog or puppy. These contracts may be very simple, or they may contain pages and pages of complex details. Remember the contract covers the sale of a living being, subject to living conditions and environment, personality and personal opinions. There is almost nothing black and white in raising a dog. For every training technique, there is a contradictory opinion. Dogs which do not fit in with one family may fit nicely with another. Even veterinary opinions may contradict each other. Hip Dysplasia, for example, can come from either a genetic problem or an injury, or a combination of both

— so who is responsible? Some contracts try to spell out everything and others leave much to the reasonableness of the buyer and the seller.

Some breeders may insist that certain puppies be shown as part of the buying contract. Be sure to inquire about show contracts if you are seeking top quality. The sale of bitch puppies sometimes includes a demand for puppies back to the breeder as part of the purchase price. Think about this carefully. You will be obligated to work with the breeder for many years to come and committed to breeding a

litter of puppies in the future when you may not want to do so. These kinds of contracts can get very specific and need to cover all kinds of details and eventualities which you may not even be able to imagine at the time you buy the dog. If you are buying a male and the breeder "just wants to keep breeding rights on him," be sure all the details are spelled out. For example, who will handle the breeding; will you have to take the bitch into your home for several days during the breeding; will your dog leave your family for the breeding period; and how much notice will be given? Any other questions you may have should be discussed and written in the contract as well. With these kinds of contracts it is *very* important that the personalities of the people fit so they can work together well without feeling put upon on either side.

If you are interested in showing or breeding the dog, you need to be honest about that up front. Today, AKC will allow breeders to mark papers as "non-breeding," which means that even though the dog or bitch may carry AKC papers, puppies from that animal may not be registered, even if bred to another AKC registered animal. You, as the new owner, cannot change the registration after the purchase. This has been instituted to try to eliminate much of the backyard breeding. Every year more breeders choose this option for their pet puppies.

Ask the breeder about spaying and neutering contracts. Ask to see the sale contract. Most good breeders will have a contract for their puppies. Look carefully for clauses which may obligate you in ways with which you may not feel comfortable. Individual breeders may add conditions which affect your relationship with the breeder and your dog for years to come. One condition that many of our breeders require to some degree or another is that the puppy have early training. Especially if you are new to Great Danes, it is worth the effort you will put into this training. Recognize that your breeder understands your puppy and what he will need to know in order to grow into an adult dog who is a responsible member of society.

Ask what guarantee the breeder offers with the puppy. CAUTION: If you are seeking a show dog, don't expect a breeder to be able to pick out a group-placing dog at eight weeks of age. These are few and far between, and a show dog is a product not only of his gene pool, but of environmental factors in his upbringing, how he is shown and conditioned, how he is presented in the ring, where he is shown, and what other dogs he is showing against on any given day. All a breeder can do is identify a quality prospect based on the pedigree and how the puppy looks in comparison to others from that bloodline. The more winners that have been produced in the past from the breeding, or from similar breedings, the better the chances of getting a winner, but don't expect the breeder to guarantee the success in the ring that often takes years to attain. Remember, if you are looking for a show ring winner, find a pedigree where the parents, other litters and other dogs in the pedigree have excelled in the ring. A good pedigree may not guarantee that every puppy in the litter will be a winner, but it gives you a good chance.

Better yet, find an older puppy or young adult that can be evaluated in the ring before you buy. Many of our breeders say that straight front shoulders, toeing in of the front feet, and improper neck sets are the most common show faults in the breed right now. The Great Dane carries two thirds of its weight on the front quarters and therefore the front needs to have proper angulation and be strong and true to ensure good movement and balance. These faults are difficult to correct in a breeding program, and often they cannot be identified until the dog is full-grown. How well a dog will show is not possible to determine until that time when his structure is clearly visible, and he has developed the personality and attitude which can make or break a winner. If you are really looking for your first show dog, older pups or even full-grown dogs are good alternatives since you already know what they will look like. Even for pets, the advantage of an older dog is that most of the growth problems have passed, health problems have shown up, and temperaments can be evaluated.

If you visit a kennel, look at other adults to get an idea of what the breeder likes. How consistent the dogs are within his kennel will often tell you how successful he is at reproducing the kind of dog he likes. See if these dogs look and act like the kind of dog you want. See the dam and, if possible, the sire of the litter. These are all usually a good indication of the quality of the puppy.

BUYING A DOG LONG DISTANCE

Sometimes it is necessary to buy a dog from a long distance. Don't panic. When you talk to the breeder on the phone, use the same technique you would use in person. Ask questions that will give you an idea about the experience of your breeder, how he or she feels about issues in the breed that are important to you and your family, how well he listens to what you want to use the dog for, and how well he tries to match you with what is available. Find a breeder who enjoys his dogs, who knows what his bloodlines will produce, and who sounds like someone you can trust and have confidence in. Ask about guarantees and expectations. You should follow the same procedure as you would with a local breeder, or one whose kennel you visit to see a litter.

If you like what you hear, and feel that you will get a good

puppy from this person, go ahead and buy the pup and have it shipped to you. Great Dane pups ship well and will arrive safely, ready to adapt to their new home. Read the chapter on shipping and travel, but realize that it is better to get the dog which is right for you, even if he must be shipped, than to settle for an inferior puppy in a short visit to a local breeder. Although most of our breeders feel that shipping is safe and reasonable, some of our breeders are opposed to sending a puppy by plane. If you are looking for a puppy from some distance, be sure to ask the breeder how he feels about shipping.

WHAT NOT TO ASK A BREEDER

Don't ask a breeder what he thinks of another breeder by name. Ask the breeder how he sees the breed or questions about his own dogs. Ask for a reference if he has nothing available. But when you begin to ask about another breeder by name, you may get more information about the politics within the breed and personal prejudices, both for and against, than real information about the quality of the dogs being bred by the other kennel. One breeder may like a certain type of dog and have nothing good to say about another breeder's dogs because they differ in style — without really giving the reason for the negative comment.

Remember also that dog breeding and showing are competitive. Over the years, disputes arise over wins and losses, or over personal matters that may have nothing to do with the quality of the dog or the purpose for which it was bred or what you want in a pup.

Do not expect to be able to come out to a breeder's home for a Sunday visit if you are simply looking at the breed for future reference. While some breeders have this kind of time, not all quality breeders do. Most of them show or compete in working events on the weekends, or they are dedicated hobby breeders who hold down other jobs and concentrate on their dogs rather than making dog sales. They will probably not have hours to spend on people who visit as something to do for the day.

Do not expect to handle a litter of puppies even if you are ready to buy. Many diseases are transmittable through handling, and the breeder may have no way of knowing to what you have been exposed. A breeder may ask you to only look at puppies. Breeders do not have the kind of inflated prices, nor the callous approach, which would allow them to simply write off the death of a puppy from overhandling or being exposed to something a visitor may

be carrying unknowingly.

Do not expect to view a litter shortly after birth. Most breeders will limit viewing to puppies which have been weaned. While it is a good idea to see the dam and the sire if possible so that you have a good idea of what the puppy may grow up to look like, strangers around very young litters (under five weeks) may irritate the bitch, and unless you are very familiar with the bloodline, you will probably not be able to see anything more than a cute lump.

If you have waited to visit until the pups are ready to go home, don't expect to get first choice in pups. Many good breeders have reservations on their pups either before they are born or from shortly after the litter is whelped. Buyers who have placed their confidence in the breeder and his reputation have put a deposit on certain pups, which have been matched up with their new homes by the breeder. This does not mean that you will not get the "best" pup for you. Each pup and each new owner will be different. It is the breeder's job to match them up as well as possible.

Finally, if you are looking for a show dog, do not take your pup or young dog to a show and ask other breeders what they think of the animal you have purchased. Trust your breeder, or don't buy from him. Remember that dog showing is not only highly competitive, it is subject to opinion. Many a good dog, in any breed, has gone back to the breeder because some new owner has taken it to a show, and listened to the opinion of other breeders — some of whom were motivated to say bad things about the entry simply because they did not want to compete against it! Your breeder knows the show game, his bloodlines and what a good dog should be. If he has shown for any number of years, he has a good feel for what will finish and what will not. *Most* of the dogs which are returned under those conditions *are* finished by the breeder as many of them have simply needed to mature and have gone on to become top winners.

WHAT A BREEDER MAY ASK OF YOU

Besides questions about your household, the breeder will want to know if you have any plans for training, exercise, and socialization. It is your responsibility to develop the potential of the pup as he grows and matures. The breeder will make recommendations based on what he feels are the needs of the breed and this pup in particular. He will ask you about other animals in your home and what experience you have had with dogs in the past. He may ask you about your willingness to assume the financial obligations which owning a large dog will entail.

Most breeders ask that you have the puppy checked by your local veterinarian so that everyone can feel confident about the health of the puppy. (Do not expect most veterinarians to be experts on the finer points of conformation.)

A breeder may ask you to call and let him know how the puppy is getting along as it grows. Remember, sending a photo of the puppy in his new home and again as an adult is a very nice thing that most of our breeders say they wished people would remember to do.

WHAT A BREEDER SHOULD OFFER

Look for a breeder who is enthusiastic in talking about his dogs. A good breeder has put a lot of time and money into his breeding program. It is natural that he or she will talk freely and with knowledge about the pedigree, the individuals he owns, and about the breed in general.

A breeder should offer a kennel pedigree of the dog. AKC will provide a certified copy of the actual pedigree for a fee, but breeders will usually give at least a hand written copy with the puppy. This is not a certified pedigree, but it should be accurate based on the breeder's kennel records. Champions should be marked.

A breeder should give you a record of the shots and worming for the puppy. Puppies should not leave a breeder without at least one set of shots, and most breeders automatically worm puppies. Puppies, like babies, put everything in their mouths so they easily pick up parasites.

A breeder should offer instructions on what to feed the pup and how to care for it. Remember that no breeder is infallible. Even with the best of care and knowledgeable breeding, some puppy, sooner or later, will have a health or temperament problem. Breeders will usually not refund money or assume vet bills, but many breeders will work with you to replace or exchange a puppy with a problem. Guarantees usually are less broad on an adult dog because

health, temperament and conformation problems are easy to identify.

One legitimate reason many breeders do not give money back is because of the attitude a money back policy promotes. The breeder wishes his puppy to become a member of the family. If breeders were to offer money back, they would be functioning as a savings bank, allowing the dog to be returned for the purchase price any time the new owner felt he no longer wanted the dog, or if he needed money. If the purpose of the buyer is truly to own a nice dog, then replacement is the logical solution, still giving the owner what he wanted in the first place — a loving, healthy pet. Another reason for the no-money-back policy is that the best breeders are usually hobby breeders who often do not have the cash flow to refund the purchase price.

Remember that even though you are buying a puppy, the purchase is more like adopting a member of the family than like buying a new car. You are not dealing with a business selling a product to a customer, but a reputable breeder who cares about placing his or her puppy in an environment which will be good for both the puppy and the new family. A reputable breeder is more like a social worker than a profit-and-loss business person. He does not make his living breeding dogs, and he is not at a buyer's disposal as a business is at the disposal of its customers. But he will be concerned about your family, finding the right dog for your family, and helping you to have a happy and rewarding life with your new dog. Please remember to treat a breeder accordingly.

HEALTH

*H*ereditary problems are a fact of life with almost all dogs. Again, one reason to buy a pedigreed dog from a good breeder is that you have some idea what kinds of health problems you may face, and how likely they are to show up in an individual animal. To think that there will be no health problems in any dog you buy is like thinking you will raise a child without ever having to take him to the doctor. By looking at what problems are found in the breed and deciding how frequently they occur and if you can cope with them as they arise, you will be prepared before you buy a puppy for what you may encounter.

ORTHOPEDIC PROBLEMS
HYPERTROPHIC OSTEODYSTROPHY (HOD)

Bone and growth problems are unfortunately common among Great Danes. The most common is Hypertrophic Osteodystrophy (HOD). Out of 4,000 cases of bone disorders studied in Great Danes, HOD accounted for more than half. The majority of these were attributed to nutrition, usually from an animal consuming more calories than was needed.

The onset of HOD is usually between twelve weeks and seven months of age. Pups have been reported with HOD as young as six weeks of age. HOD is generally observed in the front joint/growth plates, which may be enlarged, hot and very tender to the touch. Another early indication is a very close or pinched rear movement because of a soreness in the stifle or hock joints. Later, the pastern may drop, feet may splay (toes will spread apart) or feet may begin to point outward. In advanced cases, the back may roach (curved as in a greyhound) with the rear legs tucked up under the body, making movement strained and the dog look deformed. Sometimes a fever may accompany the problem; it is often misdiagnosed as an infection and antibiotics given. This treatment is not always a good idea, as some antibiotics make the problem worse or may cause allergic reactions which in turn intensify the HOD.

The best method of diagnosing HOD is radiography. The encouraging news is that, when properly treated, most cases respond to treatment. The cause is often traced to nutrition, including high vitamin supplements, too many calories, and/or dog food with protein levels higher than 24%. The treatment is to lower the caloric intake and protein levels, sometimes to as low as 17%. Ice packs on swollen joints seem to reduce swelling and ease discomfort as well as reducing fever in the area. Pups will respond within a few days, with recovery within three to four weeks. Regular, light exercise is recommended, but not vigorous or prolonged activity.

Because of this and other problems, most breeders recommend *not* feeding Great Dane puppies high protein puppy or growth formula dog foods. Senior adult or maintenance adult dog foods with 17% - 23% protein are best. The ingredients should be of good quality, not based on corn or soybeans, but meat meal, well fortified with necessary minerals and vitamins.

Several of our breeders mention feeding lamb or rice based foods, though there was a wide variety of recommended diets. Low salt dog foods, and those with levels of fat between 10% to 14% were also mentioned by more than one of our breeders.

OSTEOCHONDRITIS DISSECANS (OCD)

Osteochondritis Dissecans (OCD) is a condition normally found in the shoulder and though showing up as early as four months, it is usually seen between seven and nine months and up to fifteen months of age. It accounted for about an eighth of the cases out of the 4,000 studied. With OCD, a small flap or piece of cartilage partially or completely separates from the bone, causing great pain for the animal when moving around. It can happen from an injury but the survey suggested the weakness may be caused originally from nutritional problems. The problem can also occur in the hock, stifle or elbow joint. Some of our breeders suggest that this condition is more common in males than in females.

One of the symptoms is a limp which lasts more than three or four days. OCD must be radiographically diagnosed. Although there has been some success in treating cases—which are not severe or are detected early—with a drug called Adequan, surgically removing the detached cartilage is recommended to allow the animal to move about and live a pain free life. Since the key to recovery is early detection, the owner must pay close attention to pups during this developmental stage.

PANOSSTEITIS (PANO)

About as common as OCD, Panossteitis (Pano) usually effects puppies from five to twelve months of age. Although the disease does not cause the drastic deformation that can come with HOD, it can be the most frustrating to deal with as it frequently goes away, then recurs. (One of our breeders says the recurrence was usually the night before a dog show!) Pano is called wandering lameness or growing pains because different limbs may be affected at different times and to different degrees.

Treatment is usually changing dog food. Even low calorie/protein dog foods differ in the types of processing they use for different ingredients. There are many schools of thought on the proper balance, and many breeders believe some of the natural remedies are best. We discuss holistic medicine as an alternative at the end of this chapter. If your dog has a problem with recurring lameness, contact your breeder, and gradually change dog food, staying within the low protein/calorie range of good foods. Regular, light exercise is recommended, but not vigorous activity.

CANINE HIP DYSPLASIA (CHD)

Probably the most commonly discussed health problem in the breed is Canine Hip Dysplasia (CHD). It is very common among Great Danes, and you will probably have trouble finding a line which is completely free of the problem. The term covers a number of different deformities of the hip joint, which may or may not cause physical pain and crippling to the dog at some point in his life. Dogs can be radiographically dysplastic, meaning that their hips will not pass the hip evaluation from a set of X-rays, without ever having any physical problems, but because of the size of the Great Dane, physical signs such as lameness and pain are more common than in small breeds. The Orthopedic Foundation for Animals (OFA) keeps a registry for all breeds and will evaluate X-rays of any dog over a year old, and although a dog must be over two years old to receive an OFA Number, preliminary OFA evaluation may be done before two years of age. In some cases, OFA is a matter of controversy. While many breeders swear by OFA, others criticize it for failing to collect data on parents, nutrition, previous health, environment and exercise during critical periods of a dog's life. As a result, OFA has failed to compile the kind of meaningful data that might shed some further light on the problem. And although there are specific criteria for evaluating X-rays, there is a wide variety of X-ray equipment, technical skill, and the dog's cooperation, all of which affect the quality of the X-ray and the evaluation. Many dogs which are radiographically dysplastic, will never be physiologically dysplastic, meaning that they will never show signs of pain or discomfort from this condition. The type of dysplasia, the musculature and body build of the individual dog, and his lifestyle and exercise routines all have a lot to do with whether the dog will actually experience pain.

Whatever its shortcomings, many Great Dane breeders have supported the efforts of OFA and have made a concerted effort to improve the quality of the hips in their breed by breeding sound dogs to sound bitches. Many of the dogs in our Hall of Fame have listed their OFA numbers, and many more have OFA numbers which may not be listed on the pedigrees reproduced in the Hall of Fame. It is only in recent years that AKC has begun to list OFA numbers and keep track of them, making them part of AKC records and public records of dogs. Therefore, dogs which were registered before that information was included do not carry their OFA number on the pedigree even though they may have such a number. Be sure to discuss this point with your breeder and see how he addresses the issue of Hip Dysplasia in the breed, what his feelings are on OFA, how clear their line is of hip problems, and how frequently his dogs turn up physically dysplastic. Also find out about the guarantee if the dog is dysplastic and what measurement of dysplasia will be used. A dog with Hip Dysplasia may be able lead a long, happy and useful life, but it should not be bred.

LUXATING PATELLAS OR RUPTURED CRUCIATE LIGAMENT

Another painful and crippling condition is luxating patellas, or an associated problem, ruptured cruciate ligament. The kneecap, or patella, is located only on the back leg, and should fit into a groove, held in place by the cruciate ligament. When the patella does not fit securely, it can pop out of the groove and cause temporary or more permanent lameness until it either pops back in or is put back through surgery or massage. The ligament may rupture and cause pain until it heals. Luxating patellas may show up as early as eight to ten weeks, so it is a good idea to ask the vet to check carefully when he does the original exam on your pup. A ruptured ligament may occur with movement, sudden twisting, or loss of footing. In puppies, running through the house and slipping on slick floors, or worse yet, throw rugs which give way when the dog pushes off of them, may cause this painful condition. If this happens frequently, the ligament may stretch to the point where surgery is required. While both patella and ligament surgery are almost always successful (though costly), careful monitoring of the puppy will help prevent the problem. There is some debate whether these conditions are hereditary. Some lines do seem to have more problems than others with patellas and/or ligaments. But, since both problems are often a result of physical agility, energetic enthusiasm for life, and heavy structure, it may be that the dog's activity and attitude cause him to behave in a way more likely to encounter the problem than a dog from other, quieter lines.

CERVICAL VERTEBRAL INSTABILITY (CVI)

Often referred to as "Wobblers Syndrome," CVI occurs in many large breeds. The condition involves the lower cervical vertebrae and results in varying degrees of spinal cord compression. The afflicted dog becomes wobbly in his hindquarters. In the later stages of the disease, the dog may not be able to support his weight. The rear end begins to develop a swaying, stumbling gait. This condition was for many years considered an inheritable condition, highly recessive in nature. Recent studies have indicated that it may also be attributable to overfeeding, but much controversy still exists on the subject. Unlike Doberman Pinschers, where the disease comes on late in life, sometimes after the dog has already been bred several times, Wobblers shows up before the Dane is fully mature and ready for breeding. Breeders who find a high percentage of this condition in a bloodline usually will stop breeding that part of the line which is affected.

Treatments include using Prednisone in mild cases, surgery and in some severe cases, euthanasia.

FRAGMENTED CORONOID PROCESS (FCP)

This is an elbow defect that affects young, rapidly growing dogs in many giant breeds, manifesting itself when an area of growing bone does not fuse in the normal way. FCP is the most common cause of degenerative joint disease and arthritis in the elbow. A similar condition can be the cause of one type of hip dysplasia. As FCP progresses, there is increased lameness and marked decrease in the range of the elbow motion. Success of treatment often depends on early diagnosis and treatment which includes rest, aspirin, increased vitamin C, and in severe cases, surgery.

GROWTH PATTERNS AND PROBLEMS

Several of our breeders mentioned "stress periods " or "windows of growth." These times are especially difficult for pups of most giant breeds. Great Danes are fragile, not only physically, but in handling stress, which increases some of the problems. If you intend to raise a Dane pup, you will need to be careful with him until he is full-grown, knowing him well enough to be able to spot even the slightest deviation in behavior or development. Many breeders felt that a study of problems occurring in the breed indicates that problems of bone, skin (see below) and even temperament occur grouped around these windows rather than being spread out evenly over the first two years of the dog's life.

As mentioned, HOD is often evident during the two-to-three month window or stress period. Another window, ensuing between six and nine months, is a time when pups seem to be very susceptible to injury. This is also a time when OCD is likely to begin. Finally, the teenage period, from fourteen to eighteen months, can be difficult because of problems such as Pano, Wobblers, Hip Dysplasia, heart problems and the onset of heat cycles and sexual maturity. Personality changes often transpire during this period and an owner is well advised to be especially firm and consistent about behavior and temperament during this stage.

CANCER

It should not be surprising that bone cancers are the most common type of cancer found in Great Danes.

BLOAT AND GASTRIC TORSION

During the past twenty years the incidence of bloat in all large and giant breeds has increased dramatically. Forty years ago this problem was rarely seen in dogs. Today it frequently occurs even in medium size dogs with deep chest cavities, such as Chinese Shar-Pei. Although theories abound, we really know very little more about bloat and gastric torsion than we did twenty years ago when it began to be a common problem in giant breeds.

Not only do we not really know what causes it, but we really don't know how to prevent it. Recommended preventative measures include: feeding the dog in a quiet, non-stressful environment; limiting water right before or right after eating; keeping lots of fresh water available during the rest of the day so the dog does not feel that he needs to over consume; limiting exercise an hour before and two hours after meals; making diet changes gradually over a period of three to five days; feeding only well soaked dogfood instead of dry food; and feeding the dog in two or even three smaller meals instead of one large one. (These recommendations are also made by the Morris Animal Foundation, which has been devoted to the study of bloat for a number of years.) Of course dozens of different suggestions are made by our breeders about what kinds of food are best at reducing bloat. With a life threatening problem so difficult to pin down and prevent, it is no wonder that Great Dane breeders have developed a multitude of preventive measures. Bloat is dreaded because it occurs suddenly, and prompt action must be taken in order to save the dog's life.

Bloat begins when the dog's stomach fills with gas, food or a combination of both which for some reason cannot escape. Normal stomach action ceases and gases build up. Sometimes (but not always) the stomach "torsions" (twists), cutting off the blood supply. The dog becomes apathetic and weak. The abdomen begins to distend and becomes hard to the touch. Breathing is shallow, the front legs are spread apart, the back is often roached or humped, and the dog salivates or drools profusely with a sticky, frothy white substance. The dog may pace, thrash, look repeatedly at his stomach or show other signs of discomfort. If you open the dog's mouth, you will see that the gums are pale or a bluish color. The dog may quickly go into shock.

TAKE YOUR DOG TO THE VETERINARIAN IMMEDIATELY! Sometimes there is not much time and the survival of your dog depends on how fast you can get him medical help. In some cases a tube can be passed down the windpipe to allow the gas to escape. In other cases surgery will be required. In recent years a number of new procedures have been developed to help the problem. Stomach tacking procedures have come into use which have proved successful in preventing further problems of torsion or twisting of the stomach. A dog who survives a first attack of bloat is likely to get it again unless the stomach is tacked.

Some of our breeders recommend putting about 30 cc of a liquid antiacid like Maalox or Mylanta down the dog immediately to make him more comfortable while you are getting him to the vet. Note: Not all veterinarians perform bloat surgery or keep abreast of new procedures which are being developed. If you own a large dog, find a vet ahead of time, discuss with him the procedures he uses and get his advice on what course of immediate action you should take. Be sure he is available at any time (or has a competent emergency service) and that he is not too far away.

SKIN PROBLEMS

DEMODECTIC MANGE

In the three-to-four month age range, not only are bone problems a threat, but the stress of vaccinations, rapid growth and general socialization can cause demodectic mange to "erupt." This is a common problem with a number of breeds. The demodectic mite is present on all dogs and technically is passed from the dam to the pup. But the mite only becomes a problem when an animal's immune system is not resistant to the effects of the mite, causing hair loss and scaly patches. In severe cases, sores, pimples or small puss pockets may occur. The tendency to lower immunity during times of stress is felt to be inherited, and it can come from either the sire's line or the dam's line. Therefore, when a vet suggests that demodectic mange came from the dam, he may be both correct in the literal sense of the word, and incorrect in placing the source of the problem. This explains why you can take a dog to two different vets and get two very different opinions.

Demodectic mange can be treated by Mitaban, a commercial preparation which kills the mite. Often the problem will simply cure itself as the pup grows and his immune system becomes stronger. Talk to more than one vet, call your breeder, but do not become alarmed and discouraged if the problem occurs. Most dogs develop normally after a bout with stress and a lowered immunity and once they are fully mature it will not return.

ALLERGIC REACTIONS

Many skin problems are caused by allergic reactions, but by far the most common cause of skin problems is an allergy to fleas. For some reason people often tend to deny that their dog has fleas as if it is somehow a reflection on their home and care. In certain areas of the country, fleas are an ongoing battle, especially in the summer. Just because you don't see a flea doesn't mean that they aren't there. Regular spraying of the house, yard, and dog will keep the problem under control. Once a dog gets a flea bite, especially if he is allergic to them, an infection may begin. Scratching with a dirty paw may lead to a bacterial infection, and the moisture from licking the area may lead to a fungus infection. At that point, any single treatment will not help because you are really dealing with several problems at the same time. The easiest approach is to keep the fleas from irritating the dog to begin with. If you see black specks on your dog, usually at the point of the shoulder, at the base of the tail, on the stomach, or chest, he has a flea problem. Some of our breeders recommend using flea dip, diluted according to the package directions, in a pump spray bottle as a good solution, rather than sprays.

OTHER MINOR PROBLEMS WHICH MAY OCCUR

Great Danes have long, hard tails which are not well padded with hair. They wag them frequently and sometimes clear off the coffee table in the process. Unfortunately, when the tail strikes hard surfaces such as doors or tables, a problem may develop which is commonly called a "tail wacker." The tail may experience hair loss and sores or bruises may develop. In some cases the tail may split open, bleeding profusely. Bad tails are slow to heal because they are continuously being struck again. This is not a life threatening problem but a new owner should be aware of the possibility.

Shoe boils on the elbow are common because of the size of the dog and its weight. Technically, this is a form of bursitis which is caused by some kind of trauma which may be no more than the dog simply pulling his feet out from under himself and flopping when he lies down on a hard surface. A soft swelling develops which is often painful. If left untreated it can become a serious infection and turn into a hard mass which resists treatment. Take the dog to the veterinarian, who will remove the fluid and usually inject cortisone and/or an antibiotic into the area. Surgical removal may become necessary in some cases. Providing the dog with a soft surface to lie on is the best preventive measure.

Hard surfaces can also lead Great Danes to develop calloused areas on their elbows, hocks, and hips. The weight of the dog pressing against the ground rubs off the hair and eventually a callous begins to develop. Once established, calluses are difficult to get rid of and are unsightly, though certainly not life threatening. Soft bedding and the application of skin softener at the first sign of hair loss are the best preventive measures.

INBREEDING AND LINE BREEDING

Many people have come to blame health problems in modern breeds on line breeding and inbreeding. The problem is that many health problems are carried on recessive genes. It is possible that both parents may carry the gene for a certain health problem, but it would not show up in either one of them, because it was recessive. Yet, when they were bred together, the problem would show up in 25% of the puppies because both parents carried the recessive gene.

When a breeder does a line breeding, all he is doing is doubling up on the gene pool. If the gene pool is strong, he keeps it from being invaded by recessive genes he does not want. If it is full of unwanted genes which carry health, conformation or temperament problems, when he breeds close relatives he will have a higher percentage of pups with the problem because he is repeating the genetic pattern by breeding a stud to a bitch from the same gene pool. Thus line breeding — the breeding of a dog and a bitch with similar pedigrees and several relatives which are the same — may actually ensure that a problem will NOT occur, if the breeding is done with a bloodline which does NOT carry the problem. Inbreeding (the breeding of a sire to daughter, dam to son, full or half brother and sister — in short, two dogs which are VERY closely related) may produce a litter which is simply a repetition of what the breeder is trying to produce. However, the closer the breeding, the higher the likelihood that recessive traits will match up between sire and dam, and that puppies produced will exhibit these characteristics. Since recessive traits need to be carried on both sides in order to exhibit themselves in the puppy, the closer the breeding (repeating the same recessive traits over and over again), the more likely any given recessive trait will exhibit itself in the puppies. The same is true, though to a lesser extent, for line breeding. The difference between line breeding and inbreeding is only a matter of how closely the animals are related, and how often, over several generations, they are bred back to the same gene pool.

If a line is free of health problems, line breeding and inbreeding ensure that the puppies will be clear because there is no way for the recessive, offending gene to enter the gene pool. This is the argument breeders use for not outcrossing (introducing a new bloodline which may carry the unwanted recessive gene). But if the gene pool carries the offending gene, line breeding and certainly inbreeding will increase the chances of it turning up. Because recessive genes are impossible to identify by looking at the dog, breeders often do test breedings of close relatives to see if the trait will show up. In this way, they find out what is in their gene pool.

Although line breeding and inbreeding are part of the intricate study of genetics, and something breeders spend their lives learning about, it is sufficient to realize that the practice is no better and no worse than the quality of the stock from which the breeder started breeding. In itself, the practice does not mean that the puppies will be healthy, or unhealthy, crazy or calm, large or small. It simply means that whatever recessive genes are lurking under the surface, the tighter the breeding, the more likely they are to manifest themselves in puppies. Because of this function of line breeding, breeders who find a dog they like will often line breed to preserve the traits or "style" they like. It is their way of producing uniform dogs, that is, ones that all look alike in desirable ways when they are grown.

PUPPY SHOTS

Your puppy will come to you with vaccinations. But be prepared that these days, with rapidly mutating virus strains, the pattern of vaccinations may be different than it was a number of years ago. Some breeders begin to vaccinate very early. Others use several different vaccine combinations and give them at different times. There are several new vaccines on the market, all claiming different properties.

Get a copy of the kind of shots and the dates the puppy received them, and take it to your vet. If your vet comments about the shots, remember that vaccination schedules are becoming more controversial every year, and that veterinary medicine is not an exact science. There are opinions and beliefs, and not all vets or breeders will agree. Our suggestion is to find a vet with whom you feel comfortable, and then fall into line with whatever he suggests. The fact is that puppies survive and prosper under a number of different programs; the important thing is to be sure that vaccinations are given.

Traditionally, puppies were given a combination vaccination at eight weeks, twelve weeks and sixteen weeks. Today, many breeders are beginning shots at five or six weeks. It is safe to say you should *never* take home a puppy that has not had at least the first in the series of vaccinations.

It is important to understand that vaccinations are given in a set of three not because it takes three doses to build up the immunity, but because of timing. All pups are born with maternal antibodies. This immunity, given by the mother to the puppy, will wear off sometime between eight and sixteen weeks, but there is no way to tell exactly when. If a shot is given while the mother's immunity is still effective, the puppy will simply throw off the vaccination rather than developing an immunity on his own. Thus, it is possible that a puppy which was given a vaccination at eight weeks, but whose maternal immunity did not wear off until twelve weeks, could be exposed to a virus at, say fifteen weeks, and would have no immunity at all, because the mother's immunity prevented him from developing antibodies on his own when the original shot was given. The reason for the series of shots, is to ensure that the puppy is never left too long without either the dam's immunity or the opportunity to develop antibodies on his own from a vaccination. Thus, no matter what shots a pup has received from his breeder, you will ALWAYS need to be sure he receives his final shot AFTER sixteen weeks of age in order to ensure that he has the antibodies he needs.

"Puppy shots," or combination shots, are DHLP+Parvo (Distemper, Hepatitis, Leptospirosis and Parainfluenza plus Parvo vaccines all together in one shot). Some breeders also give Bordatella and/or Corona vaccines, and some no longer give Leptospirosis.

Rabies vaccinations work much the same way, except that only the mature shot is given. Some states and vets require that shot to be given at four months of age. Others are of the opinion that four months is too young, and prefer to give the rabies vaccination after six months of age. Although DHLP and other vaccinations may be given by breeders, every state except Texas requires that rabies vaccinations be given by a veterinarian.

All dogs should be vaccinated again at one year of age and every year after that for the rest of their lives. Rabies shots should be given according to state laws, which vary in length of time a rabies vaccination will be considered "good."

Most of our breeders recommend that you do not expose the puppy to any other dogs until after the final puppy shot at four months of age. This means that he should not visit friends and relatives with dogs, and he should not go to public parks, walkways, or any other area with heavy dog traffic. Even after inoculation, the titer (immunity in the blood) does not reach safe levels for approximately ten days after the vaccination is given.

Ask your local vet about Heartworm, Lyme Disease, and a worming program which is right for your area. Climates, weather conditions, and geographic locations make these vary from one state to another, and even from one area of the state to another. If you are buying a puppy from a warm, humid climate, the chances are that he may have worms. This is not a reflection on the breeder. Even with a conscientious worming program, breeders in the southeast may have more problems with parasites than those in the hot, dry areas of the west, or in the cold northern states.

Heartworms are a problem across the country now. There are a number of different types of medications for prevention. Treatment of an infected dog is costly and stressful on the dog. Prevention is much easier. When the dog goes in for his yearly health care and shots, he should be wormed and checked for heartworm. Ask your local vet what he recommends for treatment of heartworm in your area. Heartguard Plus is one good option, as it treats all kinds of worms at the same time it prevents heartworm. Be aware however, that this medication is given in relation to the weight of the dog. Great Danes are very large and the dosage may be expensive, especially if you have more than one.

SELECTING A VET

One of the most important decisions you will have to make is selecting a vet. Like doctors, not all vets are alike in their attitudes and treatment programs. Don't be alarmed if your breeder does not accept everything your vet may say about a puppy. Veterinarians have training in the health care of animals. They may have practiced for years in small animals or even specialized in dogs. But the breeder sees that particular bloodline, both the good and the bad, the healthy and the less perfect specimen over generations and over years. He often knows that particular animal far better than any vet who is seeing it for the first time and is judging by unrelated individuals or even unrelated breeds. Some knowledge comes with working with the same genetic pool for many years.

Although many vets are careful professionals, breeders have some recommendations in selecting a vet. If your vet begins to make sweeping generalizations about the breed and your dog — especially on the first visit — think twice about what he is saying. Most vets are not experts in specific breeds. They usually have only a working knowledge of breeds according to the dogs of that breed they have seen in their practice. Vets see unhealthy dogs more frequently than they see healthy ones. A healthy dog only comes in once a year for his regular inoculations, while an unhealthy specimen may be in the office frequently. Therefore, he may begin to base his opinion of the breed on the limited number of dogs he sees on a regular basis without realizing that there may be many more specimens that he seldom sees because they are perfectly healthy. If your vet begins to recite the health problems your pup will probably develop, especially if you have discussed these issues with your breeder and feel comfortable, don't argue; simply find another, more positive vet who knows what problems a Great Dane may have and feels comfortable treating them.

Finally, if your vet has recommended costly or unusual treatments — *get a second opinion.* This is simply good medical practice for humans or for dogs. And don't get the second opinion from another vet in the same office. People who work together often take the same approach to a problem. This tendency makes for good working conditions, but it does not give a true second opinion.

HOLISTIC MEDICINE AS AN ALTERNATIVE

Recently, people have become very interested in natural healing alternatives commonly referred to as "holistic," "complementary" or "alternative" medicines. Several of our breeders suggest natural alternatives in the areas of nutrition and chiropractic treatment for Great Danes. Several also feel that Danes have a greater sensitivity to many drugs and infections than other breeds. Sensitivity to anesthetics, tranquilizers and even some vaccines seems to be well documented. For these reasons, natural remedies have gained some popularity among those who live with and love Great Danes. However, many owners are confused about these alternatives.

Acupuncture, chiropractic, nutrition, herbs and homeopathy are the most widespread alternative therapies available. The interest is expanding rapidly into the world of pets. Conventional medicine follows a reductionist philosophy, focusing on what is considered the exact location or cause of disease and attempting to kill it, remove it or suppress it. For example, antibiotics are used to kill germs, tumors are removed or destroyed and allergic reactions are suppressed with drugs.

Practitioners of holistic or alternative medicines feel the problem is that none of these therapies address the real reasons the pet is sick. Healthy animals do not get serious infections, tumors or allergies. A pet's immune system is malfunctioning BEFORE these "diseases" occur. Therefore, what needs to be addressed is the functioning of the ENTIRE body, mind and spirit of the pet. Through this approach, the whole body functions better and can prevent or cure almost anything, according to those who practice holistic medicine.

A wide variety of holistic remedies have been used on Great Danes to varying degrees

of success. There are a number of breeders and owners who believe the health of their pets has been improved with such practices.

Vaccination has become a focus for some practitioners of holistic medicine. Noting that some Great Dane puppies develop the diseases for which they have recently been inoculated, some believe that elimination of such vaccinations is an alternative. Other breeders prefer to space out their vaccinations, or not to give them in combinations. Some breeders believe that annual boosters are not necessary, especially for dogs with other medical problems. The serious followers of holistic medicine feel that good nutrition and homeopathy can prevent these conditions as well as, if not better than, vaccinations. **IT IS IMPORTANT TO NOTE THAT SIMPLY FOREGOING VACCINATIONS IS NOT THE ANSWER.** *If you are interested in holistic medicine, take the time to learn more about it and tailor it to your dog, his needs, and your ability to provide the necessary program.* Holistic medicine as a prevention of disease is based on maintaining good health through a number of different applications, *all* of which must be carefully maintained in order for the program to work!

Nutrition - The wide variety of opinions on dog nutrition has often led to conflicting nutritional programs. Food preservatives have been blamed by some for some allergic reactions. Others feel that pets suffer as a direct result of inadequate and even toxic pet foods. Still others feel that food must be fed as it is in nature — RAW and including organs and glands, bones, vegetables, live digestive bacteria and active enzymes. Almost all of these schools of thought hold that natural nutrition can improve virtually any condition and by itself cure a great many. Additives, such as those mentioned in our Shopping Arcade section, have been found by some breeders to improve the quality of life, from improving temperament and energy levels to eliminating skin or immune problems. Allergic dermatitis of all sorts, especially prevalent in Great Danes, has often been traced to foods. Other problems found in Great Danes which have responded to diet include kidney problems and disorders of the digestive tract, including colon problems and malabsorption.

Acupuncture - Acupuncture has been used for thousands of years on humans. The life energy of the body (chi) flows through a series of channels (meridians). This energy is responsible for maintaining health and body functions. The energy may become excessive, deficient or blocked. There are points along the meridians through which the energy flow can be adjusted, usually through the use of needles. Lasers and pressure (acupressure) may also be used. Balancing and restoring energy flow can result in tremendous health benefits. With the improved health, diseases are eliminated.

Chiropractic - The central nervous system is a major communications system within the body. Interference with nerve function can result in a tremendous number of symptoms. Physical and emotional stresses cause misalignment of spinal bones and impeded nerve communication. Chiropractic adjustments restore proper nervous system function, resulting in the elimination of a variety of health problems. There is another benefit to chiropractic that is not often discussed. Three acupuncture meridians (see above) run along and beside the spinal bones. Therefore, realigning the spine allows better energy flow.

Herbs - There are different systems of herbal medicine in use: Chinese, Western and Ayurvedic (from India). The Chinese and Ayurvedic approaches focus on the energy of the body. Different herbs are used to balance the body. The Chinese system attempts to balance Yin and Yang, the opposite types of energy within the body. If the body is too Yin, the herbalist balances it with Yang herbs and vice versa. There are also herbs to strengthen the life energy (chi) and cleanse and nourish the body. Western herbs focus more on the physical body. The herbs nourish and/or cleanse the body, thereby strengthening its ability to heal.

Homeopathy - Homeopathy is a system of medicine which is nearly 200 years old. According to the law of similars, disease is cured by stimulating the body with an energy remedy. The remedy is derived from a substance which, if given in large doses, is capable of producing the same symptoms the patient is experiencing. For example, homeopathically prepared onion (allium cepa) may be given if a patient is experiencing tearing eyes, watery, irritating discharge from the nose and a desire for fresh air. Most people would recognize these symptoms as those produced when exposed to the vapors of cut onions. However, these symptoms may also occur in someone with hayfever. The cause is not important. How the individual responds is what counts. This approach results in individualized remedy selection based on the patient, NOT

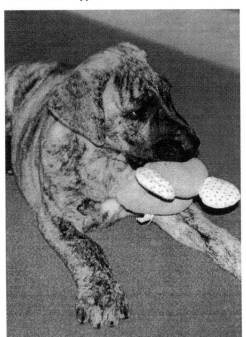

THE DISEASE. The treatment of arthritis in ten dogs may require a different remedy for each one.

These are only a few of the holistic alternatives available. Others include massage, Bach flower essences, bio-magnets, scent and color therapy. The practitioners of all of these systems recognize the individual as a whole body with a mind and spirit, not as a liver or kidney problem. They realize that only the individual can heal himself. However, the healing mechanisms must be allowed to operate unhindered. Holistic healing methods maximize healing functions and remove existing impediments.

Other varieties of holistic medicine include a balance between holistic and conventional medicine. First aid, basic health, nutritional balance and remedies based on vitamins, minerals, trace elements and herbs are used to keep the dog healthy, improve his immune system and prevent common ailments before they develop. It is important to take the time to understand the process and to tailor it to your individual pet's needs.

BRINGING HOME A NEW DOG OR PUPPY

When you have selected your new dog, you need to get ready for its arrival. Decide who in the family is responsible for the care, feeding, exercise and discipline of the dog. Decide what rules the dog and the members of the family must live by. Great Danes adapt to a routine. They will learn that one member must arrive home before they can go on their walk. They will learn sounds of cars which belong in the family, and who is a regular visitor. They will learn where and how to go out to the bathroom, and when food will be provided. It is good to decide on a pattern of care before the dog or puppy arrives. Great Danes do love to play and get human attention, and they will be loving toward the entire family if everyone is involved with them at some level.

If you have purchased a puppy, be aware that he will need several beds as he grows up. He will go from about twenty-five pounds to over one hundred. Obviously a full size bed is too large to give the puppy the feeling of a cozy nest, but a bed which is just the right size when you

bring him home will be too small within a month or so. One breeder suggested using a box or a small wooden fruit crate when he first arrives, filled with old shirts (with any buttons removed) instead of a shiny new dog bed. This homemade version gives the pup the scent of the humans in the family as a comfort. As the pup grows, just get a bigger box and add another T-shirt, but hold off on buying him a really nice bed until he is past the puppy chewing stage! An older dog, of course, can move right into his new, full size bed, but even then would probably appreciate the scent of his new owners as a way to get acquainted.

Decide where the bed should be placed. It should be in a well used, easy to clean room. Most breeders suggest the kitchen since it is often the center of family activity. Be sure that he can be contained and does not roam in areas where he is unsupervised. Pups love to explore and get acquainted. Make sure that his quarters are free of hazards and then let him explore as much as he wants.

Great Dane pups are very heavy and clumsy. They frequently lie down by simply collapsing in a heap. Be sure they have a soft bed, since they are quick to develop unsightly callouses on their elbows if they spend too much time on hard flooring. Don't play with your pup on slippery floors. He can be injured when his feet slip out from under him as he tries to make a turn. Such falls, although comical, can cause permanent damage.

During these first few critical months, nutrition, socialization, exercise, vet care and puppy training should be on the top of your priority list. If you have purchased a full-grown dog, it will be much easier. A low protein maintenance dog food will be all that he needs for nutrition, the permanent shots have been given, and he has had basic training and socialization. All an older dog needs is some consistent rules, a place to stay and people to love, and he will

make the adjustment and be part of the family within just a few short weeks.

If you purchase an older dog, be aware that although the dog may be housetrained in his old surroundings, it may take several days or even weeks to adjust to the new family and new sur-roundings. Give him time to adjust before you over-whelm him with atten-tion. Be kind, yet firm in the rules. It is kinder to establish what you expect of him from the begin-ning than to let him adjust and then to impose rules once he has become comfortable. Once he adjusts, the older dog will be ready to join right in with the new family, to travel, to visit and meet friends and to play with preteen or teenage children. He does not require as much time, training or care as a puppy.

Puppies are like babies. A puppy will need time to grow up and he will take much more than a couple of weeks to be housetrained. He will chew, may dig, and will carry things around. Great Danes mature fairly slowly and it will take him a year and a half to two years to grow up. Like a baby, it simply takes him time to get rid of some of his exuberant puppy energy, learn manners, and behave like a companion should behave. Judgment on what is his and what is yours, how to please you, and how to use his energy will take time and maturity. Don't become discouraged or angry with him. The occasional mess is simply a part of owning a dog or raising a puppy and should be expected and accepted before you purchase a dog.

Traveling with a puppy takes a little more time and preparation. To help prevent him from being carsick, don't give him food or water immediately before you leave. Many pups will still get car sick. They may throw up or drool constantly in a moving car. Most of them outgrow it by the time they are five or six months old. Riding in the car is a good idea so he will get used to it, but be sure the trips are short enough so he does not become too tired.

Puppies are fun. Friends and family members may be tempted to overpower a puppy, exhaust him, and even lower his resistance. Give the pup time to get adjusted to his new environment. Do not allow friends and family to carry him around to the point of exhaustion. Also, he should not go out where he will come in contact with other dogs until he is old enough to have a strong, mature immune system.

If you have a dog already, be aware that your older dog may dominate your new puppy. Do not allow your new puppy to be kenneled or fed with an older dog. The puppy could be permanently ruined by a strong-willed dog. No matter how kind the older dog may seem, he may dominate the younger dog.

On the first night home, whether you have picked up the pup or had him flown in, be prepared for him to be lonely. It is likely he has never been away from his littermates. He may be lonely when the lights turn out. He may cry or carry on. Be firm but understanding. Establish a routine from the beginning. Discuss ahead of time with your breeder or family how you intend to handle this behavior.

Most of our breeders strongly recommend using a crate to housetrain, or to establish a pattern with either an older dog or a puppy. Contrary to some popular opinion, many dogs love crates. A crate is their cave, or their home. Dogs, like their ancestors the fox, wolf and coyote, like the feeling of a "den," and the most successful doghouses are not huge structures, but small, enclosed areas that allow for "nesting." If you are buying a crate, be sure to get one big enough for the dog to live in as an adult, but not too big. One which is too large allows the puppy to soil it, and one which is too small is uncomfortable. Most breeders recommend a crate 36" high, 48" long, and 24" wide. Wire or plastic airline crates are both good, though it is difficult to find the plastic crates in this size. Expect that these large crates will be expensive compared to those for small or medium sized dogs.

Use the crate with common sense. Never leave a dog in a crate for excessive lengths of time. Crating not only helps housetrain, it also allows the owner to relax and enjoy himself without worrying about the dog, watching it to be sure it does not soil the carpet, or keeping an eye out to see if it is tearing up the house. Great Dane pups are like children in that they are curious and into just about everything. They need constant supervision when out of their crates and allowed to be with the family, and they need firm discipline from the beginning, enforcing consistent rules of behavior for the household.

If you allow either a new adult or a puppy to have "accidents" in the house, you will have an even harder time breaking him of the habit later on. Never let him out of your sight until you are sure you can trust his judgment.

Ask your breeder if the pup or dog is crate trained. Many breeders are believers in crates, and all show dogs must learn to travel and stay in crates at dog shows. If the dog is an older dog who has shown, he will probably be crate trained already. If the dog is not trained, put him in the crate and leave the room, staying near the door. He will probably sit there for a few minutes, then begin to cry, whine, scratch or bark. At the first noise, intervene with a sharp "NO!" The dog or puppy will begin to associate the startling voice with his attempts to get out of the crate. Some breeders use a water pistol or spray bottle filled with clear water. When the dog or pup begins to cry, they shoot a sharp, short burst of water at the dog until he stopped. Repeating this several times with the word "NO!" makes the point a little more strongly. They also suggest using a water gun when the dog is out of the crate to stop unwanted behavior in the house such as chewing or scratching at doors.

Once he is quiet in the crate for about thirty to forty-five minutes, praise him quietly, but don't make a big thing out of this. Put him outside. Watch and see if he goes to the bathroom. If he does, praise him lavishly.

Bring him back in the house and let him play and be free for fifteen to twenty minutes. After play time, put him back in the crate and repeat the process. Consistency will help him learn through association. He should be crate trained after only a few short tries. The other lessons may take longer!

He should be able to keep the crate clean all night by the time he is three to four

months old. The more careful you are with your routine, and the more consistent, the more rapidly he will train. Never give him more time to play and be free in the house than he can handle without having an accident. But use common sense and don't leave him in the crate too much. By the time he is four or five months old, he should be fairly well house trained. The fewer times he makes a mistake, the sooner he will be a reliable member of the family.

Your expectations should be consistent and you should never encourage behavior in a pup that you cannot accept in an older dog. For example, if you do not want an older dog on the sofa, don't pull a pup up on the couch with you. If you do not want a hundred pound dog jumping on you when he is older, don't let a pup jump. It may be cute when little puppy paws reach your knee, but it is not so much fun when a grown Great Dane puts his paws on your chest and looks you in the eye — if you are still standing! For example, a pup may stare at you, then if you hold his stare, snap at your face. This is funny with an uncoordinated puppy, but not funny at all in an adult dog. If it will be dangerous and unpleasant once the dog is grown, don't let the puppy do it. If you do not think the behavior is appropriate for an adult dog, *DO NOT LET THE PUPPY BEGIN THE BEHAVIOR.* Correct him sharply with a "NO" when he starts it. It is much harder to break bad habits than to establish the ground rules to begin with.

Feeding schedules should find a routine which is convenient for both you and the dog, but which is consistent from day to day to promote housetraining. Remember, it takes six hours for food to go through a dog. Feed him, then walk him or let him out for exercise on a regular basis. A puppy must be fed three or four times a day, depending on his age and established patterns. This schedule can gradually be reduced to twice a day by the time he is six months old, and once a day for an adult. Regular exercise in the form

of walks or playtime will also help regulate his system. Always let him out just before you leave the house and the last thing at night. After a while he will get used to the routine and realize this is his last chance to go to the bathroom before having to spend time in his crate. This routine will help encourage him to eliminate and reduce the likelihood of soiling his crate.

Before you bring the new dog or puppy home, be prepared. Find out what the breeder is feeding and what the feeding schedule is. Get food and water bowls of appropriate size (elevated so he will eat about shoulder height) and decide where to put them. Stainless steel bowls are usually the preference of breeders as they are easy to clean, can go through the dishwasher to be sterilized, and cannot be chewed, chipped or splintered.

If you are using a crate, be sure it is convenient to move around, even if it needs to stay up most of the time. A bed or blanket may be good indoors, while outside, a box with shavings may be better. A bored Great Dane will almost certainly drag a blanket all over the yard, and may even reduce the large blanket to several small ones! Blankets in dog houses will be dragged outside the doghouse and shredded, as will any kind of a pillow or foam bed. When the dog is in the house, he usually has his "house manners" and will be more willing to appreciate his bed, pillow or blanket in one piece. However, don't leave him alone for long periods of time until he is older and more mature or you are likely to find he has made some alterations of his own to cabinets and furniture.

Toys or chew bones are good to have on hand, but they should be large. The rawhide chew bones with a knot on the end are preferred by breeders over the flat chips which become soft and may choke a dog if swallowed. There are a number of good chew items on the market today.

Most of our breeders recommended against leaving a collar on a dog, especially a puppy. Small feet may get hung up in them, or they may become hooked on something in the house or yard. Put the collar on when you are taking him on the leash, and remove it before you leave him unattended, even in the crate. Collars also can ride up and bother the cropped ears.

If possible, arrange to pick up your new dog or pup at a time when you will be staying home for a few days. Friday may be good, if you have time on the weekend to spend with him and help him get used to you as a new owner.

Your puppy should be at least nine weeks old, and should have his ears cropped already. If you are new to cropped-ear breeds, cropping and ear care can be a difficult time. Even finding a qualified veterinarian who knows Great Dane crops can be a problem. All breeds have a slightly different style of cropping, so a veterinarian who is used to doing American

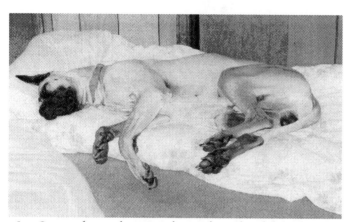

Staffordshire Terriers, for example, may or may not be knowledgeable in cropping a Great Dane, which has a much longer and more elegant cut. Many vets do not like cropping or do not like to do it, or they take little care with it. It is therefore better if the initial arrangements, the cropping and the primary ear care have been done before your puppy comes to you. This means that the breeder must invest more time

Great Danes are heavy and sometimes clumsy. They need a soft bed to keep them from developing unsightly callouses.

and money in the puppy, but good breeders will be happy to do it in order to ensure their pups get off to a good start.

Your pup should be bright eyed, with a loose skin which looks two sizes too big for him. His coat should be shiny and his feet a little too big for him. Expect him to be uncoordinated with his long colt legs and interested in everything around him.

TRAINING A DOG YOU CAN LIVE WITH!

Good training and exercise seem to be the hardest thing for pet owners to understand and give their dogs. Virtually all our breeders recommend obedience classes. Great Danes are very good in obedience work in the ring, but even if you never intend to show, obedience classes help you raise a well mannered dog. Early training is very important. Without it, a problem dog can develop and problem dogs are the ones who end up in the SPCA. No breeder wants to think of his or her puppy ending up in a rescue situation. Breeders say over and over again that proper socialization — that is, exposing the dog to strangers and a wide variety of situations as well as spending quality, loving time with him at home — is the biggest single factor which will ensure success. One breeder says the time it takes to housetrain and leash train, and whether a Great Dane is neurotic as an adult, all depend on the consistency and care of early training and socialization. Time invested in a puppy is invaluable in producing a good dog, and lack of time invested as a puppy is very difficult to make up once the dog is an adult with bad habits or a neurotic personality.

KEEP IN TOUCH WITH THE BREEDER

A good breeder's job does not stop when the puppy goes home. Call the breeder when you arrive home or when the dog arrives by plane to let him know that everything is fine. Call him in a few weeks and discuss any problems or rewarding experiences you have had with your new family member. Send a photo whenever you can. Feedback helps breeders evaluate their breeding programs, and most of them truly enjoy hearing news of their "children."

Sometimes, because of changes in lifestyle or family pattern, it becomes necessary to find a new home for the dog. If so, you should contact the breeder BEFORE you give the dog away to a new home or take him to the SPCA. Many breeders require this notice in their contracts, but we suggest that you make the effort to contact the breeder under such circumstances, whether or not it is mentioned in your contract. Good breeders are interested in their dogs, and they wish to follow them throughout their lifetimes.

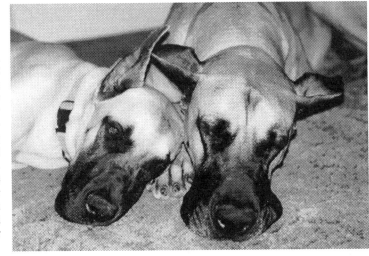

THE PAPERWORK

*T*he term "AKC registered" has meant, up until a few years ago, that a dog simply had a dam which carried AKC papers and a sire with AKC papers, both of the same breed. In turn, it could be bred to any other registered dog of the same breed, and the puppies could be registered. Any dog with two registered parents was eligible for registration and breeding, regardless of its quality.

In recent years, AKC has responded to pressure to put some limit on the number of breeding dogs in the general population. Since 1991, dogs may be marked by their original breeder as "non-breedable." This designation means that the dog will be issued papers from the AKC with a gold, rather than a purple border. If such an animal is bred, even if bred to a dog or bitch with a regular purple bordered certificate with full breeding privileges, the puppies produced will not be eligible for registration.

When you buy a puppy, the breeder should give you two papers. The first, a kennel pedigree, will be on some kind of paper with a "tree" of names, like those in the "Hall of Fame" section. This pedigree lists the sire, dam, grandparents and so on of the puppy. It will look something like this:

```
                                              grand sire of sire
                           sire of sire
                                              grand dam of sire
             sire
                                              grand sire of sire
                           dam of sire
                                              grand dam of sire
YOUR DOG
                                              grand sire of dam
                           sire of dam
                                              grand dam of dam
             dam
                                              grand sire of dam
                           dam of dam
                                              grand dam of dam
```

The registered name of a dog is often in two or three parts. The kennel name of the original breeder usually begins the name, followed by the name of the individual dog, and finally a second kennel name may follow if the dog was purchased as an unnamed puppy by another breeding kennel. This practice dates back to the early years in England when dogs were referred to by their owner's name first, because names in those days were very simple and duplication of names for dogs in the field was common. To make reference easier, people began to refer to the dogs as "Lord Grimstone's Susan" or the "Duke of Hamilton's Sam." These, combined with the year of their whelping, comprised the early pedigree records.

Today a dog may be named, as with the dog on page 71, "Ch. Darce's Shaka of Champlain." The name shows that the dog named "Shaka" was bred by Darce Great Danes, owned by Joan Byas and Dorothy Eggebrecht (the Ch. before the name designates that he has earned his championship title), and was purchased as a puppy (before registration) by Sharon Day of Danes of Champlain, who added her own kennel name at the end of the dog's registered name. Thus the dog is "Ch. (the championship title earned through dog shows) Darce's (designating the breeder) Shaka (the individual dog's name) of Champlain (designating the owner at the time the dog was registered). He later became the foundation dog for the Danes of Champlain. A slight variation of this is on page 68, where BISS Ch. (the titles earned by the dog) Alano's

(the kennel which owned the bitch at the time of registration), Anastasia (the name of the bitch), of Maitau (the breeder), appears In this case the name of the purchasing kennel was put in the front, while the name of the breeding kennel was put at the end. She is nicknamed "Ana."

Dogs bred and still owned by a breeder at the time of registration will carry only a kennel name, usually in front of the individual dog's name. On page 75 of our Hall of Fame, "BISS Ch. Meadowood's I'm Stormin' Norman" was bred by Gisela Wood of Meadowood Estate Danes, who also bred the dam of this dog, and if you look at the pedigree, the grand dam (each of these bitches carries the kennel name "Meadowood," with no other kennel mentioned). The individual dog's name is "I'm Stormin' Norman."

As explained on page 63, dogs who compete successfully earn titles which stay with them throughout their lives. Only conformation championship titles precede the name. Unless otherwise specified, "Ch." refers to an AKC title. Some dogs will have abbreviations of countries which indicate that they have earned conformation championships in more than one country. (Can/Am Ch. — would be Canadian, American Champion.) BIS or BISS is not technically a title. It means that the dog has won Best in Show, or Best in Show at a Specialty (a show where only Great Danes are showing).

Other titles follow the name of the dog. These include working titles, obedience titles and other levels of achievement, including the latest AKC title of recognition — CGC — Canine Good Citizen. Learn more about titles in the section on competition.

The BLUE litter registration will enable you to register your dog. Fill it out, including the name chosen for your dog in the boxes provided. Fill in the color and the back of the form and send it to AKC for your dog's registration. THIS IS NOT YOUR REGISTRATION - AND YOU ONLY HAVE ONE YEAR FROM THE DATE THIS APPLICATION WAS ISSUED TO BE ABLE TO REGISTER YOUR DOG!

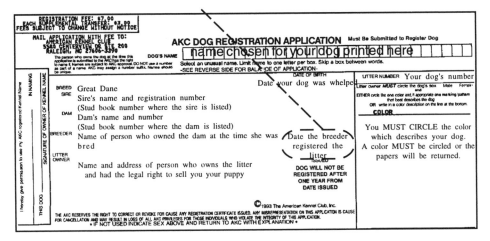

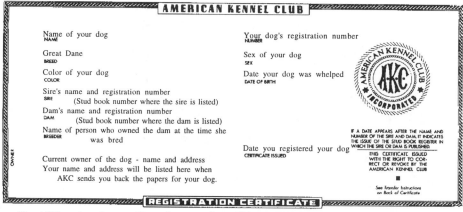

AMERICAN KENNEL CLUB

Name of your dog
NAME

Your dog's registration number
NUMBER

Great Dane
BREED

Sex of your dog
SEX

Color of your dog
COLOR

Date your dog was whelped
DATE OF BIRTH

Sire's name and registration number
SIRE   (Stud book number where the sire is listed)

Dam's name and registration number
DAM   (Stud book number where the dam is listed)

Name of person who owned the dam at the time she
BREEDER   was bred

IF A DATE APPEARS AFTER THE NAME AND NUMBER OF THE SIRE AND DAM, IT INDICATES THE ISSUE OF THE STUD BOOK REGISTER IN WHICH THE SIRE OR DAM IS PUBLISHED.

Date you registered your dog
CERTIFICATE ISSUED

THIS CERTIFICATE ISSUED WITH THE RIGHT TO CORRECT OR REVOKE BY THE AMERICAN KENNEL CLUB

Current owner of the dog - name and address
Your name and address will be listed here when
AKC sends you back the papers for your dog.

OWNER

See Transfer Instructions on Back of Certificate

REGISTRATION CERTIFICATE

The AKC registration certificate for your dog will be issued when you fill out your blue puppy registration and submit it to AKC with the required fee, or, if you have an older dog, when you transfer your dog's registration to your name.

When you buy a puppy, it is possible that a breeder may not have the AKC papers back, especially if the puppy is very young. But you should get some kind of kennel pedigree, at least a note that assures you the puppy is registered.

If the breeder has the puppy registrations, they will be on blue paper. Be sure it is filled out completely. THIS IS NOT YOUR REGISTRATION CERTIFICATE. Ask your breeder about naming your puppy. Some breeders insist that pups be named with a certain letter of the alphabet to help them track their pups throughout the years. Sometimes this can lead to funny and awkward names, especially if the letter is "X", "Y" or "Q!" Other times they will require that a word or idea is included in the name. Look to see which box is checked regarding the breedability of the dog. Be sure the breeder has signed as owner of the litter. Finally, be sure that "sex" and "color" are checked on the front of the puppy registration form.

ACCORDING TO AKC RULES which only have been in effect a few years, YOU MUST REGISTER THE DOG WITHIN ONE YEAR OF THE TIME THE PUPPY PAPERS HAVE BEEN ISSUED, or it cannot be registered. Therefore, it is important to take care of the paperwork as soon as possible.

Keep your kennel papers if you have them. If they were not provided, you can get a certified copy from AKC, or use a pedigree service such as the one mentioned in the Shopping Arcade Section. Canine Family Tree will provide you with a complete pedigree, usually faster and less expensively than AKC. If you intend to breed your dog, you will most certainly need to know what is "behind" him or her. You will need to make inquiries about the strengths and weaknesses of these ancestors, and what will be most likely to match up with your pedigree to produce good quality puppies. If you intend to hire your male out for stud, bitch owners will ask to see a copy of the pedigree. If you wish to take your bitch to a stud for breeding, most stud owners will ask to see the pedigree before they agree to use their stud. They will want to look for lines with known health problems, and lines that will or will not match with those of their stud.

Even if you never intend to breed, it is worth the investment to send for a copy of the complete pedigree. Champions of record will be marked in red, and you can see what famous dogs are in your dog's pedigree. You may enjoy matching the pedigree with those listed in the "Hall of Fame" sections, not only looking for particular individuals, but familiar kennel names.

The AKC registration certificate is 8.5" X 4" with a purple border and the official AKC incorporation seal. It will list the current owner and breeder. It also lists the name and number of the sire and dam. The small number in parentheses after the registration number (i.e.: 1-88) is the month and year of registration. It will NOT list the pedigree beyond the sire and dam of your dog. Send this information, and the dog's registration number (or simply send a photocopy of the registration certificate) to the pedigree service or AKC for the complete pedigree.

If your dog is older and has already been registered, you will need to follow the "transfer instructions" on the back of the registration certificate. Fill out the back section A completely, be sure section B has been signed and send in the fee and the ORIGINAL CERTIFICATE. AKC will issue a new certificate, with you listed on the front as the owner.

If your AKC certificate comes back with a gold border, your dog has been marked "non-breedable" and puppies produced from him cannot be registered, even if bred to a pedigreed mate.

COLOR IN THE GREAT DANE

O ne of the most important concerns for Great Dane breeders is color. The Breeders Color Code of Ethics as endorsed by the Great Dane Club of America addresses the issue of color breeding. Fawns may be bred to another Fawn or a Brindle only, and a Brindle may be bred to another Brindle or a Fawn only. Harlequins may be bred to another Harlequin, Harlequin-carrying Blacks (that is, Blacks with Harlequins in their ancestry), or Blacks from a Black breeding. Harlequin Blacks may only be bred to Blacks from a Black breeding, Blacks from Harlequin breedings or Harlequins. Blues may be bred to Blues, Blacks from Blue breedings or Blacks from Black breedings. Blacks from Blue breeding may only be bred to Blacks from Black breedings, Blacks from Blue breeding or Blues. Finally,

These uncropped pups are examples of a "Boston" marked Black (front) and a "Piebald" or reverse Boston (rear).

Blacks from a Black breeding may be bred to any color except Fawns or Brindles. (See Color Breeding Chart, below.) Most breeders believe that all colors shall be pure-color bred for four generations and that color mixing other than that set forth in the Color Code of Ethics is injurious to the breed.

In Great Dane colors, there are two factors: color and markings. One of the problems with Great Danes is that there are a number of different patterns which occur within the breed, even with carefully bred dogs. A Boston, for example, is a marking pattern. It refers to the white which runs down the face, around the neck, and up the legs. This pattern is common among other breeds, most notably the Boston Terrier and including Boxers, Staffordshire Bull

COLOR BREEDING CHART	Fawn	Brindle	Harlequin	Black from Harlequin	Blue	Black from Blue	Black from Black
Fawn	X	X					
Brindle	X	X					
Harlequin			X	X			X
Black from Harlequin			X	X			X
Blue					X	X	X
Black from Blue					X	X	X
Black from Black			X	X	X	X	X

This is an example of a Boston marked black. This color is legal for show in Canada, but not in the United States.

Terriers and many herding breeds. Less common, but possible from color mixed breedings, is Fawn with Boston markings. The Boston pattern is not acceptable for a show in the United States, but was recognized a few years ago by the Canadian Kennel Club, and Bostons are shown in Europe. Another pattern also considered a mismark is a reverse Boston where the dog is white with a black head and sometimes tail (often referred to as piebald).

Harlequin also refers to a color pattern. Although black and white is the only recognized combination, the Harlequin pattern may include merle spots, brindle spots or, in the case of mixed color breedings, even fawn spots. A poorly marked Harlequin may be simply over-marked. That is, it has a large black blanket on the body, a solid black leg or legs, or black patches over the entire body, including the neck, chest and front legs. Some have very heavy black color with what seem to be white patches on the black body. Under-marked Harlequins are mostly white with few, if any, black patches. Sometimes these dogs only have black marks on the head and face, or they may have many small spots like a Dalmatian. Pet-marked Harlequins may have a dirty white color with a lot of black hair in the white areas.

Black, Fawn, Brindle, Blue and Merle refer to colors, each of which may be found in any of the color patterns. Merle is a solid mouse-gray color or a mouse-gray base with black or white spots (or both black and white spots). The gray may also be "ticked" with white or black. "Ticking" is commonly found in English Setters and describes the presence of only a few hairs of the darker or white hair which form a small blob of color like the tip of a small paint brush. White on the chest of a Great Dane is acceptable, and more acceptable than it was twenty years ago. However, the white must be limited to the center of the chest, and should not be large or spilling out over the point of the shoulders. A speckled chest and markings on the paws are permitted but not desirable. Often, Black dogs have some white hairs or markings on them, and they may still be winning show dogs.

Accepted show colors for the United States are only Fawn, Blue, Black, Brindle and Harlequin (black and white only). There are other naturally occurring colors which may be fairly frequent especially in Harlequin litters. Litters of Great Dane pups may have several colors in them, though if they are color bred, those colors will only be the colors which are interbred since these are the only colors in the bloodline. A litter from a Fawn to Fawn breeding for example, may also include Brindle pups if there are Brindles close in the bloodline.

As described in the standard, undesirable colors include white, merle, Harlequins and solid-colored Danes in which a large spot extends coat-like over the entire body so that only the legs, neck and point of the tail are white. Also undesirable are Brindle, Fawn, Blue or Black Danes with a white forehead line, white collars, high white stockings or white bellies, and Danes with Blue, gray, yellow (Fawn) or Brindled spots. The reason these colors are specifically listed in the standard is because they frequently occur in the breed, even from some of the best breedings.

This black is typical of mismarking in blacks. There is too much white on the chest and feet to be a show dog.

Merle is by far the most common unacceptable color. Merle may be anything from very small patches on an otherwise well-marked dog, which is acceptable, to a solid

This merle pup is typical of the color, gray with both black and white spotting. There is a mixture of ticking (small spots of color from a few hairs to a spot about the size of a dime). Merle is a color often found in Collies and Australian Shepherds.

merle dog with large black or white spots, to a white dog with merle spots neither of which are acceptable.

Some breeders, in an attempt to modify head or body type, will cross color lines and make a mixed breeding. If Harlequins are cross-color bred into Fawn lines, many perversions of the patterns described above may occur such as "fawnoquin" — white with Fawn (brown or yellow) patches; or "Boston Fawn" — Fawn with white neck, chest, front legs; white rear stockings; a white tail tip and a white face blaze. These markings may vary considerably and occur only in mixed-color breeding.

Fawns and Brindles may also be mismarked, though this is not nearly as common as mismarked Harlequins and Blacks. Mismarking usually involves too much white on the chest or white on the feet and tail. Very pale dogs, ones without a black mask or Fawns which are so dark they appear to be cloudy in color, are not desirable for showing, though not actually considered mismarked. In Brindles, dogs with only a slight trace of black as Brindle stripes, or ones with so many stripes that they appear almost black are mismarked. Any dog with white on the face, other than a Harlequin, is not acceptable.

Harlequins are difficult to breed. For many years they were referred to as the hobby of millionaires because breeding them is so inconsistent. A male and female may produce a litter with three or four well-marked pups. The repeat breeding of the same male and female may not produce a single well-marked pup. A Harlequin litter will contain pups of other colors, and only about 30% of the litter will be show marked. This percentage has held fairly steady across the country and throughout the history of Harlequin breeding. Sometimes a single litter, a single bitch, or a single breeder will beat those odds, but like Las Vegas, they can just as easily be way below the average for the next breedings. All breeders of Harlequins will get pups of unacceptable show markings. Seldom does a show-marked Black come from a Harlequin litter, although it is not uncommon for Blacks to be born in a Harlequin litter. White dogs also occur, and often are deaf.

One of the reasons Harlequins tend to be higher in price is that there are fewer of them. Many show breeders will euthanize pups of undesirable color at birth, but sometimes they offer these for sale as pets. Some of our breeders feel that selling mismarks as pets is a legitimate and humane way to handle the miscolored dogs. Others feel very strongly these miscolored pups should be put down at birth, and they do not want to talk about anything but show-colored Harlequins. Although all Harlequin litters will contain poorly marked pups, some breeders feel that selling these pups will give their kennel a bad name, or they do not wish to deal with selling pet pups to non-show homes. Since a litter of Harlequins frequently contains more mismarked dogs than show-marked pups, this means finding and dealing, in some fashion, with a large number of pets.

If you are interested in a Harlequin you must decide ahead of time exactly why you

A merle dog is gray with black and/or white spots. Merles may come in any pattern from solid merle to merloquin, which is white with merle spots. This uncropped pup is a Boston marked merle.

want the dog. If you are looking for a show-marked Harlequin, go to a show breeder, one who is experienced in knowing just what a show dog needs to look like. If you are looking for a breeding dog, it should be show-marked. The reason for this is that show-marked pups may be as few as two or three pups out of a litter of eight or ten, even when breeding well-marked dogs to well-marked dogs. If you are breeding poorly marked dogs, the chances of getting well-marked Harlequins drops considerably. An ideal show-marked Harlequin has a nicely marked face, white neck, chest and front legs with medium-sized, evenly distributed black patches which look as if they were "torn" from black paper and placed upon the dog evenly from the withers down the body to the hind quarters. It should have clear white in the white area, free of black hairs, and a minimum of merle anywhere on the body.

This litter is typical of one which might occur from any Harlequin breeding. There are two black pups (although not visible in the photo, both are pet-marked because of too much white under their chests), two show-marked Harlequins, a reverse Boston or piebald (center white pup with a black head), a merle and an undermarked Harlequin (top center) which may be shown, but is not considered a desirable color.

If you want a pet and are looking for a mismarked color, be very careful about how you approach the breeder. Many breeders are extremely sensitive about this subject, and will become irritated as soon as the conversation turns to mismarked dogs. Instead of asking if the breeder has any mismarked dogs, it might be better to begin by asking what his policy is on mismarked dogs and how he feels about the subject. This gives the breeder a chance to explain his position before you commit yourself to the fact you are searching for a mismarked dog.

One of the reasons we have included mismarked colors in this book is so you are aware that they do occur and that they are not acceptable to many reputable breeders. This means that if someone is trying to sell you a pup which looks like any of the mismarked ones we have pictured here, you should be paying less, not more, than for a well-marked Dane. A very fre-

These are pet-marked Harlequins. The one on the right has too much black, including black which extends down the leg like the sleeve of a sweater. Harlequins should not have black on their legs. The dog on the left is under-marked. Although some breeders show these undermarked dogs, other breeders feel very strongly against it.

quent problem stems from unethical breeders— or backyard breeders who truly don't know what they are doing— selling these pups as "rare" colors. Buyers who do not know about the colors

in the breed frequently believe this claim because they have never seen a Great Dane in this unusual pattern. More than one breeder talks about seeing a novice owner show up at a dog show, proudly showing off his new, mismarked Great Dane and talking about how lucky he was to have found this rare dog and that he paid a very large price because it was a rare color. It is a bad experience when breeders at the show are disdainful of the dog, critical of the breeder who sold the dog and sometimes even rude about the ignorance of the new owner. The goal of this book is to inform new owners that these

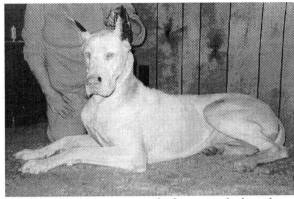

A white Great Dane is not considered a recognized color. Often these dogs lack pigmentation around the eyes and nose. This bitch is a true albino with pink eyes. Like many white Great Danes, she is deaf.

colors do exist — in fact they are frequently whelped from some of the best breedings — but they are not acceptable to many breeders, and never acceptable for the show ring.

Keep in mind, however, that a mismarked dog should not sell for practically nothing. These dogs come from the same litters as the well-marked dogs, with the same careful breeding and the same care and money put into their early lives. The breeder has still produced a quality dog, far superior to one produced by a puppy mill or backyard breeder. When he quotes a price around $500, he is taking the color into consideration because if the color were good it would be far more. Some of these dogs are very lovely, and the color rarely has anything to do with health and temperament. If you find one from a good breeder who has chosen to sell his or her mismarked pups instead of putting them down, they will be of good quality, sound in temperament and strong in conformation because they come from the same well-bred litter as their show littermates.

Because of the limited gene pool in some colors, there are some differences in temperament and style between the colors. Some of our breeders feel that Harlequins are more intense about everything. They have a reputation for being harder headed. One breeder claims they are more clinging to their people and another says she feels there is a higher incidence of skin problems. One undisputable problem with Harlequins is that they show the dirt more than the other colors because of the white in the coat. Blacks, Brindles, Blues and even most Fawns do not show dirt and grass stains and seldom need bathing. The white on

This pet-marked Harlequin has a lot of merle.

Harlequins can become stained and may need to be scrubbed with a whitening shampoo. This is not unique to the Great Dane. It is true for any breed with large areas of white.

DOG SHOWS
AND OTHER COMPETITIONS

M any a dog has lived his entire life as a companion, friend and confidant to his family without ever finding the need to have a career of his own. But some dogs do work for a living, and if they prove worthy, will earn a degree or title to attach to their names. The most common of these is a "Conformation" title from the American Kennel Club (AKC). Conformation means "manner of formation; structure; form, as a physical entity" according to *Webster's Universal Unabridged Dictionary*. Simply stated, it is what the dog looks like standing still and moving at a trot, and how well he matches the written standard for the breed. As you can see from our Hall of Fame section, dogs of outstanding quality and attitude have earned the title "Champion." ("Ch." appears before the registered name, and is used every time the registered name is printed.) Once earned, this title, like all dog titles, will stay with the dog for the rest of his life. A champion is a champion for life.

Championships are earned by exhibiting at AKC shows and collecting points. The number of points earned at each show will vary, depending on the number of dogs of that breed which are entered in competition and defeated. It takes fifteen points for a dog to be a champion, but at least twice in his life the dog must win a "Major," that is, he must earn three points at one show. This is not as easy as it might seem, since there are not many majors each year, and the dog must win the top award in heavy competition.

Points are awarded for each breed based on how many dogs are showing in the area each year. There are nine AKC divisions across the country, and the points may be different for each division and each breed within the division. Points may even be different for each sex within the same breed. For example, the chart below shows the points needed for six of the nine AKC divisions for shows held between May 1, 1996 and May 1, 1997. The Northeast includes: Connecticut, Maine, Massachusetts, New Hampshire, New York, Rhode Island and Vermont; the Southeast includes: Alabama, Arkansas, Florida, Georgia, Mississippi, Louisiana and South Carolina; the Midwest includes: Iowa, Kansas, Minnesota, Missouri, Nebraska and Wisconsin; the Southwest includes: Arizona, New Mexico, Oklahoma and Texas; and of course California and Alaska are just those states.

The points refer to the number of points earned if a given number of dogs or bitches are showing. Points are earned *only* by the top winning dog or bitch of that day's competition. For example, if you had a dog or a bitch winning at a show held in Maine, and fifteen dogs or sixteen bitches (including yours) showed that day, your dog would earn three points toward its

Location	Points	Dogs	Bitches	Location	Points	Dogs	Bitches
Northeast	1	2	2	Southwest	1	2	2
	2	8	9		2	9	10
	3	15	16		3	16	17
	4	20	21		4	18	21
	5	28	30		5	23	28
Southeast	1	2	2	California	1	4	5
	2	7	10		2	11	12
	3	13	19		3	18	19
	4	18	25		4	23	26
	5	28	36		5	33	39
Midwest	1	2	2	Alaska	1	2	2
	2	7	9		2	3	5
	3	13	16		3	4	8
	4	19	22		4	5	10
	5	30	34		5	6	11

championship (a major). But if you showed the winner in Alaska only four dogs or eight bitches would need to show that day for a major. In Wisconsin, if thirteen dogs showed, your dog would have earned a major, but if you were showing a bitch, you would only earn two points, which is NOT a major, because sixteen bitches are needed to earn three points in Wisconsin, even though it only requires thirteen dogs.

The area of the country where the show is held is the deciding factor, not the home of the dog. Thus, dog owners traveling from one area of the country to another will need to keep in mind the different point scales when computing their points.

No matter how many entries are attending a show, five points is the most that will be earned. Even if the show is a large "Specialty" (a show which has been recognized by a regional or national Great Dane Club and attracts hundreds and hundreds of entries) will still award only five points, but as you can see from our Hall of Fame, winning at a Specialty Show will be considered more significant simply because of the larger number of entries. Breeders often mention "Specialty" wins because they are more prestigious.

Breeds with fewer dogs, or breeds with fewer dogs showing, will have very different numbers. Pulik, a relatively unknown breed, showing at the same show in the same year might need only two dogs or bitches for a point, three dogs or bitches for two points, four dogs or bitches for three points, and six dogs or bitches for five points! This is because there are far fewer Pulik whelped and shown than there are Great Danes. If the breed becomes popular and more dogs are shown, the points will begin to go up each year as the number of entries rises in shows in the area. When the number of entries in a breed falls, the points will go down the following year. In this way, AKC limits the number of champions in each breed or variety to about 150 to 200 per year. A listing of points in the area can be found in the show catalog for each breed entered at the show, or you can call the AKC Event Records Department for a copy of the point system. The new point system is printed each year in April and goes out with the AKC Calendar of Events, a monthly publication listing shows across the country for the next several months.

As you may have noticed, in the world of dog shows, a "dog" is a male — and only a male — and a female is a "bitch." Classes in dog shows are divided by dogs and bitches. The top winning dog will be "Winners Dog" and the top winning female will be named "Winners Bitch." The best between them is the "Best of Winners." In conformation competition, all entries for the class enter the ring at the same time. The judge looks at the entire class standing, from the side and moving around the ring at the trot. The judge then "goes over" each entry, that is to say he looks at the teeth and puts his hands on each dog to feel its structure. Each entry is then moved at the trot and the judge looks at the movement as the dog goes away, from the side, and as the dog returns to the judge. While in the ring, dogs are to stand at attention at all times and to behave with manners toward their handlers, the judge and other dogs.

To attend a show, call your local kennel club, watch the newspapers, look in the phone book, (which often lists yearly events in the area and will sometimes list the dog shows), call the AKC Event Records Department or call your breeder. Once you are at a show, visit the vendors around the grounds. Those selling general merchandise will usually sell calendars with the shows listed in them. Some of our vendors in the "Shopping Arcade" section of this book also carry these calendars.

If you have never entered a dog in a show, perhaps the best thing to do is go and see what a show is like. Entries must be made two and a half weeks ahead of time, and a program is

(Continued on page 97)

HALL
OF
FAME

THE FOLLOWING SECTION IS A SHOWCASE FOR STARS OF THE BREED. All of the dogs pictured on the following pages are title holders. These animals will give you an idea how current outstanding individuals of the breed look and what bloodlines produce these qualities. The breeders and kennels listed on these pages represent a range of style within the breed. They have also been selected from across the country, giving you a chance to talk to a breeder in your area.

We congratulate the breeders and owners of these dogs for their dedication to fine Great Danes. Their time and effort insure the success of their dogs, and the continuation of the breed.

Here is an explanation of some of the titles you will see:

Ch. - champion — conformation titles precede the name. A listing of abbreviations of countries indicates that the dog is a champion of record in each of the countries outside the United States as listed. If no country is indicated, the dog is an AKC champion. (American Kennel Club) If a dog has a "BIS" (Best In Show), or a "BISS" (Best in Show Specialty) award it is sometimes indicated before the Championship designation. Although not formal titles, these are prestigious awards and are often used with the names and titles for the rest of the dog's life.

WORKING TITLES

United Kennel Club working titles also preceed the name. Most working titles will follow the name of the dog, as will titles of breed club recognition.

CD - Companion Dog, an obedience title.
CDX - Companion Dog Excellent, the next level of obedience.
UD - Utility Dog, the highest level of obedience title. Abbreviations of countries before an obedience title indicates that the dog holds obedience titles in each of the countries listed.
TT - Temperament tested.
CGC - Canine Good Citizen, a title awarded by AKC through a specific test of obedience and temperament.

ROM - Registry of Merit, a designation indicating a dog which has met certain requirements set out by a national breed club.

Please note that minor discrepancies in the presentation of titles are the result of breeder preference and lack of a universal protocol.

FRONT COVER DOG:

```
                         Nobile Aus Dem Eldorado
              Ch. Atlas Ad Emirat, DCH, VDHCH
                         Ch. Lana Aus Dem Eldorad, DCH, ES '83
      Quarterback Liberte (German Import
                         Ch. Gallo Von Harekin, BS '84
              Noblesse Liberte
                         Dodini D'Oro Liberte
Scarbrough Fair's Contessa
                         Konak's Huckleberry Finn
              Scarbrough's Anaconda
                         Konak's Dark Side of Moon
      Scarbrough's Amanda
                         Scarbrough's Anaconda
              Scarbrough's Claudelle
                         Scarbrough's Katrina
```

Scarbrough Fair has both bred and imported Harlequins since 1970. Our primary market is for healthy, intelligent family pets with good temperaments and small breeders who want a solid foundation on which to build. The average life span of Danes from our bloodlines is between ten and thirteen years. We guarantee health, temperament, against hip dysplasia for life and against enlarged hearts for seven years.

Arlene Scarbrough
911 Fayetteville Rd
Atlanta, Georgia 30316

Scarbrough Fair Great Danes
(404) 378-2203

REAR COVER DOG: *WYSIWYG Blue Star's Wülfgar*

Sire: Crazy Lions Yogi   **Dam: Angel Van-hets Star Sapphire**

Wülfgar was one of twelve beautiful puppies. He earned his many gray hairs over the last ten years. Wülf was never a show dog but he is a true champion in the eyes of all who know and love him. He is a successful graduate of obedience school (as all Danes should be !), and he is a loving and loyal companion. He is a true Canine Good Citizen and a wonderful ambassador for the breed. He has gone to the office with his "mom" every day of his life. He has introduced more people to the breed than we could possibly count. His intelligence has more often than not amazed strangers, veterinarians, and even his owner! Danes have earned the reputation of being very short-lived. Although this can be true, many breeders are working toward improving the life span of these gentle giants. Careful screening of breeding stock for hip dysplasia, heart and eye defects, or other genetic problems helps to insure the health of future puppies. Careful examination of pedigrees and proper selection of breeding pairs can yield not only beautiful dogs, but healthy ones as well. Much of the credit for Wülf's longevity and health goes to his owners for their careful attention to routine health care as well as their immediate response to any problem situations. Along with this it is essential to recognize and thank the dedicated individuals who have been responsible for keeping Wülf happy and healthy all these years: Dr. Vicki Fowler and Dr. Joel Edwards. Without the care and love of these very special people Wülfgar wouldn't be celebrating his tenth birthday. However, with their help and the grace of God, he will be celebrating many more.

Breeder:
Teresa K. LaBrie
WYSIWYG Great Danes
277 State Hwy 320
Norwich, NY 13815
(607) 336-9226

Owners:
Mark & Sheila Lobdell
P.O. Box 759
Averill Park, NY 12018

CH. DANE LANE'S MILTON

Ch. Rojon's Captain Fowler
Ch. Rojon's Doctor Ly
Ch. Honey Lane's Lolli Pop
BISS Ch. Rojon's Don-Sue Luke V. Lost Creek
Ch. Rojon's Oh Boy V. Mecca Dane
Ch. Rojon's Teena Marie Don-Sue
My John's Hanta Yo
Ch. Dane Lane's Milton
Ch. Reann's French Aristocrat
BIS, BISS Ch. Sheenwater Gamble On Me
Ch. Stone River 's Delta Dawn
Sheenwater Seventh Heaven
Sheenwater Herman V. Thor Dane
Ch. Thor Dane's Mindy Sue
Windeehollow Tahari V. Bodane

Ch. Dane Lane's Milton finished his championship on 9/6/93 at the age of 16 months, exactly 90 days after being awarded his first points. He is a very sound, good moving dog with a wonderful temperament and excellent brindle coloring. We have been involved with Great Danes since 1971 but did not become active in showing until we purchased our first show dog in 1985. He was Ch. Apadane's Roffe of Suedane, another brindle dog sired by Ch. Rojon's Don-Sue Luke V. Lost Creek, who is also Milton's sire. While showing is very important to us, our first priority at Dane Lane is that our dogs be part of the family. All our dogs live in the house and are pets first and show ring competitors second. Dane Lane is very proud of Milton, and we look forward to continuing to watch his show career and his offspring.

Sue and Steve Mahany
11407 North Rt. 91
Dunlap, IL 61525

Dane Lane Great Danes
(309) 243-7054

BIS, BISS, AM/CAN/INT CH. TRAVIS LINCOLN

Can Ch. Cilka's Excalibur
Can Ch. Cilka's The Boss Von Gereen
Can Ch. Sasa Dcera Sulana of Cilka
BIS, BISS Can Ch. Boss's First Son Joshua
Kimdane's Khan of Vali Hi
Can Ch. Queen de Elegence of Roy Hill
Morgana's Venus
BIS, BISS, Am/Can/Int Ch. Travis Lincoln
Am/Can Ch. Paquestone's Lincoln Legend
Am/Can Ch. Lincoln's TJ of Roulet
Am/Can Ch. Lincoln's Sierra of Fairoaks
Can Ch. Lincoln's Georgie Girl
Am/Can Ch. Lincoln's Mr. T of Sierra
Am Ch. Lincoln's Amanda of Bridlewood
Lincoln's Missy of Bridlewood

"Travis" has joined almost 40 years of breeding tradition at Lincoln Great Danes. Since 1955, we have produced over 80 American or Canadian Champions owned and/or bred or co-bred. This includes BIS, BISS, Top 20 or Group winning and placing Great Danes. Pictured above at 17 months "Travis" is a proven Stud, OFA certified and pure color bred.

Owners:
J. B. and Sandy Britts
2519 96th Ave Ct. E.
Puyallup, WA 98371
(206) 952-4061

Co-Owner:
Clare Lincoln
(206) 481-4426

BISS CH. MANATASQUOT'S JAMES TAYLOR

```
                                    Ch. BMW Brody
                        Ch. BMW Graffitti, CD
                                    Ch. BMW Impeccable
            BMW Avalanche
                                    Ch. BMW Ruffian
                        BMW Serenity, CD
                                    Ch. BMW Prima Donna
BISS Ch. Manatasquot's James Taylor
                                    Ch. Sounda's Marathon Man
                        Ch. Z-Dane's Sounda Music
                                    Ch. Z-Dane's On The Q T
            Manatasquot's Carly Simon
                                    Ch. High Acre's Beaugardas
                        Manatasquot's Bette Midler
                                    Carrousel's Graceful Lady
```

Champion Manatasquot's James Taylor — # 10 Great Dane in Working Group competition (1994) — completed his championship at 12 months of age with four majors! He stole the hearts of breeders and judges alike at Westchester K.C. (1991), winning Best of Breed from the puppy class; and once matured, taking the Breed at Westminister in 1993. Taylor's career has progressed to becoming a Best in Specialty Show winner, Group winner and multiple-group placer. He has also proven himself to be an extraordinary producer with champion and multiple pointed get, who have inherited his spectacular movement, tremendous substance and superior intelligence.

<u>Breeder, Owner</u>
S. Henley Dodge
P.O. Box 233
Blue Point, Long Island NY 11715

Manatasquot
(516) 363-6016
(800) 420-8687

BISS CH. ALANO'S ANASTASIA OF MAITAU

                                          Ch. Bodane Tourister
                            Ch. Sheenwater Ace In The Hole
                                          Ch. Sheenwater X-Clamation
              Ch. Dundane's Bacarat V Brookside
                                          Ch. Windane's Zephyr
                            Brookside's Abby of Dundane
                                          Ch. Dundane's Catrinka
BISS Ch. Alano's Anastasia of Maitau
                                          Ch. Caprata's Simba
                            Ch. Winhurst Cherokee Red
                                          Ch. Winhurst Fanfare
              Ch. Maitau's Tattletale
                                          Ch. Darrdane's Opening Bid
                            Ch. Maitau's Conversation Piece
                                          Contessa Natasha of Tarra

"Ana" began her career at 6 months with a Best in Sweepstakes and a class win at the GDC of New England Fall Specialty. She progressed rapidly, finishing her Championship at 13 months and winning an Award of Merit in 1989 at the GDCA National Specialty in St. Louis, Missouri, at only 15 months. Despite limited showing, she earned a place in the top 20 Great Danes event in 1991 catapulted by the high point in her career, the Best In Breed win at GDCA National Specialty in Chicago. Since her retirement, Ana has been true to her Maitau and Dundane heritage by producing Champions and major pointed, quality puppies excelling in soundness, type, temperament, and movement. We hope Ana's influence will continue to be seen in future generations. Handled by Terry Silver of Norfolk, Massachusetts.

Owner: House of Alano   Breeder: Maitau Great Danes
Sandy Tombari   Patricia A. Ciampa
108 Scobie Pond Road   P. O. Box 37
Derry, NH 03038   Hollis, NH 03049
(603) 434-9301   (603) 465-3368

CH. MICHAELDANE DAGON CLOROX N'CO

```
                                    Ch. BMW Ruffian
                        Ch. BMW Bull Lea
                                    Ch. BMW Fantasia
            Michaeldane Dagon's Bull's I
                                    GMJ's The Condaur
                        GMJ's The Lady Celeste
                                    Dean's First Lady
Ch. Michaeldane Dagon Clorox N'CO
                                    Ch. BMW Bull Lea
                        Ch. The Architect N'CO
                                    Ch. GMJ's The New Yorker and Co
            Replica N'Co
                                    Ch. BMW Bull Lea
                        Ringtop's Essence N'Co
                                    Ringtop's Edelweiss Von DMS
```

Rox began his show career at six months of age. At the 1990 National Specialty he won the 6-9 Harlequin puppy dog class; completed his championship at fifteen months of age and immediately went into the best of breed classes; placed in the upper 15 of Best of Breed at the 1991 and 1992 National specialities; received an award of merit in 1993 and won the stud dog class. Mid-1994, he was standing 13th among the top twenty. Sire of three champions and eight pointed dogs with get across the U.S., in Mexico, Argentina, and Japan. Producing outstanding conformation, color, and temperament.

Jodie & Bud Keim
P.O. Box 472
Sonoita, AZ 85637

Jaybee Danes
(520) 455-5236

MACY'S GLORY OF BLUE MOON, CD, TT, CGC

Willowrun's Candidate
Willowrun's Spike
Cartouche V'T Buitengebeuren
Ch. Darce's Kali of Champlain
Darce's Angus Knight of Ember
Darce's Tarnished Angel
Darce's Fall'n Angel
Macy's Glory of Blue Moon, CD, TT, CGC
Willowrun's Spike
Am/Int Europasieger Ch. Rachel's Ravon Pal V Willowrun
Willowrun's Zena of Sharcon, CD
Kennedys Alexis Alica Macy's
Ch. Haltmeier's Uno King V Hearts
Verlin's Crystal V Sapphire
Black Marmaduke

"Beauty is a greater recommendation than any letter of Introduction"
-Aristotle
Blue Moon Danes, the home of quality blues and blacks.

Anita & Richard Brown
139 Cantrell Rd.
Hazel Green, AL 35750

Blue Moon Danes
(205) 828-0407

CH. DARCE'S SHAKA OF CHAMPLAIN

```
                            Ch. Rodane's Noble Othello
                  Ch. Sancarley's Ringo Starr
                            Pasha's Tingaling Sancarley's
            Diamant Bleu of Champlain
                            Darce's Bleu  Renaissance
                  Lady Sacha of Champlain
                            Misty Blue Dawn II
Ch. Darce's Shaka of Champlain
                            Ter-ron's Octavious
                  Darce's Angus, Knight of Ember
                            Lady's Delta Queen of Darce
            Darce's  Tarnished Angel
                            Darce's Spartan Warrior
                  Darce's Fall'n Angel
                            Lady's Delta Queen of Darce
```

Danes of Champlain strives with every breeding to produce type, beauty, and excellent temperaments. Shaka was our first champion. Pictured here at 16 months, he earned his title from start to finish in two months. Bred by Joan Byas and Dorothy Eggebrecht, he was the start of Danes of Champlain. He produced both champions and pointed get. Danes of Champlain continues to produce champions and quality dogs with excellent temperaments.

Joan Byas and Sharon Day
23940 S. Loomis
Crete, IL 60417

Danes of Champlain
(708) 672-7646

BISS CH. GEMSTONE'S KAITLYN LA-DI-DA

```
                              Ch. Reann's French Aristocrat
                 Ch. Honey Lane's Go-For -It
                              Ch. Honey Lane's Do It Again
        BISS Ch. Honey Lane's Casablanca
                              Ch. Rojon's Doctor Ly
                 Ch. Honey Lane's Silvia V. Rimac
                              Ch. Honey Lane's Nut Meg, CD
BISS  Ch.  Gemstone's  Kaitlyn  La-Di-Da
                              Ch. Windane' s Zepher
                 Ch. Darrdane's Opening Bid
                              Ch.  Lyn-Dane's La-Di-Da
        Gemstone's Megan V Darrdane
                              Ch. Roo's Maxwell of Mt. View
                 Lyn-Dane's Lady Jessica
                              Lyn-Danes Lower Case JJ
```

Once in a lifetime are any of us blessed with that "special" Great Dane. I was one of the lucky ones. Kaitlyn was the first bitch in the history of the Top 20 Celebrations to be a contender for 3 years in a row. In the ring she was poetry in motion. Outside of the ring she produced quality get that are sound in mind and body. Many of these dogs are registered therapy dogs and have earned their Canine Good Citizen title. At the time of printing, one of our Shoreline girls, Cedarglades Rythm "N" Blue's is undefeated in Senior Veterans Class at the top shows on the east coast. She is ten years young. We breed for longevity and have achieved considerable success with many of our Danes living long and active lives.

Nancy Simmons
61 Cassville Rd.
Jackson, NJ 08527

Shoreline Kennels
(609) 924-3444
fax (908) 928-1392

BISS CH. PATCHWORK BENNEDANE'S CALI GIRL

Ch. BMW Bull Lea
Michaeldane Dagon's Bull'sI
GMJ's The Lady Celeste
Ch. Michaeldane Dagon Clorox N'CO
Ch. The Architect N'CO
Replica N'Co
Ringtop's Essence N'Co
BISS Ch. Patchwork BenneDane's Cali Girl
Riverwood's Ringtop Jagla
Ch. Heritages Beta Von Riverwood
Ch. Heritages's Chardonnay
Ch. Patchwork's KT Scarlet O'Hara
Ch. Koenigdane's Prince Perseus
Ch. Suschens Spirit of Christmas
Ch. Suschens Ein Kopie Der Lilli

This is BISS Ch. Patchwork BenneDane's Cali Girl. "Cali" finished her American Championship in July 1994 at the age of 17 months. She was handled to her championship by Ms. Terry Silver and acquired three Best in Sweepstakes, two Best of Breeds from the classes, one Best of Opposite, and became one of the youngest Harlequin bitches ever to finish her American Championship. Her career was crowned by winning her first Best in Specialty Show at the Great Dane Club of Des Moines in September 1994 at 19 months old. Michael Childs handled Cali there and made our dream come true. We are looking forward to breeding Cali in 1996.

Holly Bennett
P.O. Box 265
Albion, ME 04910

BenneDane
HARLES and BOSTON

BenneDane
(207) 437-2170

AM/CAN CH. WILLOWRUN'S WYSIWYG GULLIVER, CGC

Willowruns Spike
En/Int/Am Ch. Rachel's Ravon Pal V. Willowrun
Willowruns Zena of Sharcon, CD
Ch. Willowrun's Naughty But Nice
Saphir Du Val De L'Amitie
XWillowrun V'T Buitengebeuren
Fleur V'T Buitengebeuren
Am/Can Ch. Willowrun's WYSIWYG Gulliver, CGC
Willowruns Spike
En/Int/Am Ch. Rachel's Ravon Pal V Willowrun
Willowruns Zena of Sharcon, CD
Willowruns Autumn Night
Willowrun's Val's Black Gold
Slim Kittie of Merritt
BG Merritt's Willowrun

Gulliver is a color-pure blue male, born July 26, 1989. He is pictured here at age three with handler Judy Harrington, shown under judge Mrs. Eve Fisher. After earning his Canine Good Citizen title and his US Championship, Gulliver went to Canada and finished his Canadian Title in only 4 days! He has sired hundreds of puppies and has numerous pointed and champion (Breed and Obedience) get in the US and Canada. He is also the sire of International/Mexican, BIS American Champion WYSIWYG's Sami-blu O'Belldane, the first blue Dane in history to ever win an All-Breed (also all-champion) Best In Show! Gulliver lives with his owner Teresa La Brie and her husband David Kunzinger.

Breeders:
Michael and Pamela Bronson

Owner:
Teresa LaBrie — WYSIWYG Great! Danes
277 State Hwy 320
Norwich, NY 13815
(607) 336-9226

BISS CH. MEADOWOOD'S I'M STORMIN' NORMAN

Ch. Honey Lane's Go For It
Ch. Honey Lane's Casablanca
Ch. Honey Lane's Sylvia V Rimac
Ch. MJM's LeMans von Meadowood
Ch. Darrdane's Opening Bid
Ch. MJM's Class Act of Lyndane
Ch. Murlo's Scarlett O' Harris
BISS Ch. Meadowood's I'm Stormin' Norman
Ch. Rojon's Doctor Ly
Ch. Rojon's Don-Sue Luke V. Lost Creek
Ch. Rojon's Teena Marie Don-Sue
Meadowood's Dawn
Ch. Pedadane's Justinian
Meadowood's Lady Godiva
Misty Mountain's Emyn

The opening sentence of the Standard seems to have been written with Norman in mind: "The Great Dane combines in its distinguished appearance dignity, strength, and elegance with great size and a powerful, well-formed, smoothly muscled body..." Not only is he sound in body but also sound in mind, and just a joy to live with. He finished his Championship before he was a year old- with all majors- received his first BISS and Group I placement at the tender age of 17 months- Is a "Top 20" contender in his first year out as a "Special". He has sired multiple champions, and numerous, pointed and major pointed get (with limited breedings). His most endearing quality is evident in his interaction with people — big or small — he loves to be hugged and cuddled and always looks for the idle hand that could be giving him some attention.

Gisela Wood
6803 Cook Rd
Powell, Ohio 43065

Meadowood Estate Danes
(614) 761-0670

AM/CAN CH. GREYHAVEN'S ELROND V DANEHOLD

Ch. Sandale's What a Guy
Ch. Von Shrado's I'm A Knock Out
Ch. Von Shrado's Easter Bonnet
Ch. Amelor's Fly So Free
Ch. Murlo DeMarco
Amelor's Encore
Ch. Amelor's Cameo
Am/Can Ch. Greyhaven's Elrond V. Danehold
Ch. Paquestone's Lincoln Leger
Ch. Lincoln's T. J. of Roulet
Ch. Lincoln's Sierra of Fairoaks
Ch. Lincoln's Boheme of Greyhaven
Ch. Shannon's Acheeon
Lincoln's April of Fairoaks
Ch. Lincoln's Sierra of Fairoaks

American Canadian Champion Greyhaven's Elrond V. Danehold has only shown twice before September 1993, taking a reserve to a major in one of those two shows. His show career then started for real in September 1993 and he went on to earn his Canadian and American Championships by January, 1994. His Canadian Championship was earned in a single weekend taking WD at a specialty and two all breed major shows. He finished his American Championship by taking WD at two major shows and one two point show under two breeder judges during one weekend in January 1994. All his points were put on by his owner/handlers Barbara Lewellen (8 of the points) and Loise Van Alstyne (8 more points, including his majors). "Ellis" was then kept at home to gain some more maturity before resuming his show career in October of 1994. Ellis is shared by Barbara Lewellen, Tina Alvarez, and Mark VanAlystyne.

Barbara and Tom Lewellen
13240 42nd N. E.
Seattle, Washington 98125

Danehold
(206) 365-6721

CH. BROOKSIDES CECILIA, UD, TT

```
                           Ch. Ashbun Acres Avant-Garde
                 Ch. Bodane Tourister
                           Bodane Sophisticated Lady
       BISS Ch. Sheenwater Ace in the Hole
                           Ch. Sheenwater Phoenix
                 Sheenwater X-Clamation
                           Sheenwater Lily's Laughter
Ch. Brooksides Cecilia, UD, TT
                           Ch. Rojon's the Hustler
                 Am/Can Ch. Windane's Zephyr
                           Windane's April Storm, CD
       Brooksides Abby of Dundane, CD
                           Ch. Dagon Spartacus V Phyldane
                 Ch. Dundanes Catrinka
                           Beba Valeries Little Libra
```

Ceci was the foundation bitch of Legacy Great Danes. She was purchased in 1984 as my next obedience dog, however this one had show potential and an excellent pedigree. "Ceci" became my third utility titled Great Dane and the breed's first bitch to obtain a championship and utility title. She was handled in conformation and Junior Showmanship by my daughter Amy and by me in obedience and often was shown in all three classes at the same shows. Ceci was bred twice and produced nine puppies of which only five were shown. Shown out of the first litter were: Ch. Legacys Idle Wild South; Ch. Legacys Unforgettable Fire, UD, TT; and from the second litter: Ch. Legacys Legend In My Time, CD, CGC; Ch. Legacys Too Hot V. Tabordane, CD, TDX; and Ch. Legacys Living Legend. Ceci is proof that "a well balanced dog has a title at both ends." All Legacy dogs are OFA, Cardiac, Thyroid, and VWD tested.

Patricia Thurow
4378 Cox Farm Rd.
Acworth, GA 30102

Legacy
(770) 974-6650

BISS CH. ROKADANES JAHALOM NAHZEER

```
                                    Ch. Shannons Tycho Brahe
                      Ch. Corinths I Am Abel V. Hydane
                                    Ch. Hydanes Femme Fatale
        Ch. Rambos Abel Acclaims Th'Boss
                                    Princetons Icon Von Waldheim
                      Ch. Princetons Brandy Alexander
                                    Princetons Paige of Braeside
BISS Ch. Rokadanes Jahalom Nahzeer
                                    Ch. Fantas Abraham von Waldheim
                      Ch. Danehills Able Von Waldheim
                                    Danehills Lady Ginger
        Can/Am  Ch. Tigroschka
                                    Cin-Lyns C-Lancer V Lindi-Dane
                      Stasha Of Gentle Giants
                                    ISIS Of Gentle Giants
```

Holly was born an orphan puppy in December 1986, and went to Christmas dinner in a diaper bag. She had a very satisfactory show career with limited showing as a Special in 12 shows (9 BOB and 1 BISS). Afterwards she retired to the maternity ward and gave us two beautiful litters. Then when most Danes are ready to retire to the sofa, Holly again appeared in the show ring. From the competitive Veterans Class with her breeder owner, she won a BOB at a very large specialty show for her second BISS. This is truly a Dane with a heart. At Rokadane, we breed Danes to win (your Heart).

Peg Billings
61246 C. R. 21
Goshen, IN 46526

ROKADANE

Rokadane
(219) 533-7965
Fax (219) 534-7965

ROBBIES I'M SUNSHINE SUPERMAN CD, CGC

Ch. Sheenwater Georgia Pacific
BISS Ch. Sandale's What A Guy
Murlo Sybil Of Sandale
BIS, BISS Ch. Von Shrado's I'm A Knock Out
Ch. Von Shrado's Bit Of Sunshine
Ch. Von Shrado's Easter Bonnet
Ch. Von Shrado's Bit of Grenadilla
Robbies I'm Sunshine Superman, CD, CGC
Ch. Corinth's I Am Abel V. Hydane
Ch. Grenadilla's Rocky Von Shrado
Grenadilla's Aurola
Robbies I Am Sassy
Gin-Ed's Whizz Bangs Flasher
Robbies Classy Sassy V Gin-Ed
Lazycroft Sunshine Gold

Robbies Great Danes was founded December 1980. Sassy, our foundation bitch, lived to be over eleven years old. Her daughter, Porsche and her grandson, Superman not only have a competitive drive and titles to prove it, but also work to help their fellow canines by going to many nursing homes and local schools to assist in lectures on the responsibilities of dog ownership. Superman, now five and half years old, has earned his CD. He is a very smart guy and a thinker. All of my Danes have been wonderful companions and the GREATEST OF FRIENDS to me and my family. To me:

"THERE TRULY IS NOTHING LIKE A DANE!"

Janette and Roy Robinson
4100 Whitmell School Rd
Dry Fork, VA 24549

Robbies "R" Danes
(804) 724-4475

CH. SUNNYSIDE CALIFORNIA POPPY, OFA

```
                                    Ch. Reann's French Aristocrat
                        Von Raseac's French Gigolo
                                    Ch. Von Raseac's Cerissa V. Song
            Ch. Von Raseac's French Dandy, ROM
                                    Ch. Von Raseac's Chaz of Hillview
                        Hillview's Chantilly
                                    Ch. Kingswood Hillview Irish Rose
Ch. Sunnyside California Poppy, OFA
                                    Ch. Reann's French Aristocrat
                        BIS, BISS Ch. Sheenwater Gamble On Me #1 A. S.
                                    Ch. Stone River's Delta Dawn
            Sunnyside Narcissus, OFA, ROM
                                    Ch. Temple Dell's Aaron
                        Sunnyside Kiwi, OFA
                                    Ch. Sunnyside Daffodil
```

Poppy is champion number 13 for Sunnyside Farm with very limited breeding. She is a sweet and funny clown and a joy to live with! She has four champion littermates who have earned a Register of Merit (ROM) for their mother Sunnyside Narcissus and father Ch. Von Raseac's French Dandy. Her first litter of four by Ch. Bonneville Jackson show the same high quality and outstanding temperament as their parents. Three of this litter have finished and the fourth is on her way! Owner-Breeder: Jill Swedlow. Co-Owner: Brucie Mitchell.

Jill Swedlow
39887 Swedlow Trail
Yucaipa, CA 92399

Sunnyside Farm
(909) 797-1855

AM/MEX/INT BIS CH. WYSIWYG'S SAMI-BLU O'BELLDANE

```
                              Ch. Rachel's Ravon Pal V Willowrun
                  Ch. Willowruns Naughty But Nice
                              Willowrun V. T. Buittengebeuren
      Ch. Willowruns WYSIWYG Gulliver
                              Rachel's Ravon Pal V. Willowrun
                  Willowruns Autumn Night
                              Slim Kittie of Merritt
Am/Mex/Int  BIS  Ch.  WYSIWYG's  Sami-Blu  O'Belldane
                              Night Pharah's Blue Barron
                  Greystoke of Blueridge
                              Carron's Miss T. Blue
      Symbazu Starphire O'BellDane
                              Ch. Kali's Blue Print V. Mako
                  Hoppers Misty Blue
                              Atlantis Porsha Blue Moon
```

Sami finished her championship at eighteen months. At twenty-two months, she became the first Blue Dane ever to win Best in Show Honors at an all-breed AKC show and the first Dane to win Best in Show at the prestigious Del Monte Kennel Club in over fifty years. Beautifully presented by Larry Schram.

Jean M. Bell
14232 Shaffi Ln.
Castroville, CA 95012

BellDane Blues
(408) 633-3105

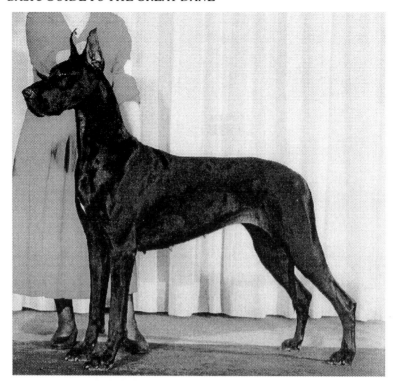

BIS, BISS AM/CAN CH. DIANA-LINK'S DANCIN-IN-THE-DARK

```
                                    Haltmeiers Uno King V Hearts
                      Haltmeiers Kodiak
                                    Haltmeiers Fortune Seeker
          Mikaldane's Master Charge
                                    Rojon's Oh Boy V Mecca Dane
                      Michaeldane's Dream Girl
                                    Jolly's Gypsy Rose Lee
Am/Can   Ch.   Diana-Link's   Dancin-In-The-Dark
                                    Rory Von Sligo of Wildwind
                      Haltmeiers Uno King V. Hearts
                                    Azurs Elbina
          Diana N Link's Blue Crystal
                                    Dianadane's The Duke of Earl
                      Link's April Love V Othello
                                    Julie's Black Scheffleras
```

Breeders/Owners/Handlers of five All Breed Best In Show Danes including Fawns, Harlequins and Blacks. Winners of the Great Dane Club of America Nationals and the GDCA Futurity Winners and holders of the record for the most top winning Great Danes in Canadian history. We strive for excellent health, temperament and conformation.

Bonne & Gayle Klompstra
RR #1
Sombra, Ont.
Canada N0P 2H0

Sheboane Great Danes
(519) 892-3389
FAX (519) 892-3369

BISS CH. HARLEY DAVIDSON HARDT'S

```
                                    Ch. Honey Lane's Let's Go For It
                        BISS Ch. Honey Lane's Casablanca
                                    Ch. Honey Lane's Syliva V. Rimac
            Ch. Maher's Top Gun V. Hardt's
                                    Ch. Darrdane's Opening Bid
                        Maher's Dream Girl
                                    Barristers Sweetie
BISS CH. Harley Davidson Hardt's
                                    BISS Ch. Sandale's What A Guy
                        BISS Ch. Von Shrado's I'm A Macho Man
                                    Ch. Von Shrado's Solitaire
            Cullinane's Holly V. Hardt's
                                    Ch. Shadam's Gideon
                        Ch. Cullinane's Estasis
                                    Ch. Joy-View's Calendar Girl
```

This elegant bitch excels in breed type, soundness, and temperament. Her classic head and effortless movement are a joy to watch! In her first two weekends shown as a "special," Harley took three BOBs and a Group III!

Owner:
Stephanie Gallups
Harley D. Danes
36286 Allder School Rd.
Purcellville, VA 22132
(540) 338-6250

Breeder/Handler
Tonie Gerhardt
Hardt's Danes
4515 Twinbrook Drive
Fairfax, VA 22032
(703) 764-3755

CH. GLEN-GLO'S KARMA, UD, TT, CGC

BMW Winston Churchill
Ch. Chauffeured's Dr. Levy JR
Chauffeured's Coalette
Ch. Glen-Glo's Shaman
Ch. Glen-Glo's Goodtime Charlie
Ch. Glen-Glo's Ladyhawk
Ch. BMW Glen-Glo's Chi Chi
Ch. Glen-Glo's Karma, UD, TT, CGC
BISS Ch. Coogan's Winterhawk
Ch. Glen-Glo's Goodtime Charlie
Empress Von Fina of Nightwind
Glen-Glo's Onyx Orchid
BISS Ch. Coogan's Winterhawk
Glen-Glo's Lady Athena
Glen-Glo's My Girl Funnyface

Glen-Glo's breeds for soundness and balance, with beautiful movement, above average intelligence, true athletic dane type and temperament, but most important to us is general overall good health and longevity. The Great Dane is a gentle giant, first and foremost a loving pet, and a great companion. We love the breed in all its colors but have a special interest in the hardships of breeding the Harlequin.

Glenn and Gloria Bearss
7062 Kermore Lane
Stanton, CA 90680

Glen-Glo's Great Danes
(714) 995-3121

CH. DAVISDANE PHOTOGRAPHER

Ch. Heritage's Beta Von Riverwood

BISS Ch. Patchwork's Ashley Wilkes

Ch. Suschens Spirit of Christmas

Davisdane's Jordan

Ch. Davisdane's Snapshot

Ch. Davisdane's Picture Perfect

Laurenwood Sweet Rosie O'Davis

Ch. Davisdane Photographer

Ch. Davisdane's Double Exposure, CD

Sir Maxwell Thor Davisdane

Maitau's Miladi Charro

Davisdane's Off the Richter

Ch. Davisdane's Snapshot

Davisdane Oreo

Laurenwood Sweet Rosie O' Davis

Ch. Davisdane Photographer is the sixth Davisdane Champion. He was handled primarily by his breeder/owner Susan Davis. Davisdane began in the summer of 1976 when Stanley Davis bought his wife, Susan, a Harlequin puppy as a housewarming gift. Susan began exhibiting the dog and, although he never finished his championship, his gentle nature and outstanding conformation instilled in Susan a love and appreciation of the breed. Several Harlequin champions and obedience title-holders followed. Among those were Ch. Davisdane's Double Exposure, CD; Ch. Davisdane's Snapshot; his daughter Ch. Davisdane's Picture Perfect; Ch. Amherst-Davisdane Roadrunner; and Ch. Davisdane Photographer. A lovely Boston sister to Picture Perfect, Onarok's Focus on Davisdane, was taken to Canada and completed her Canadian Championship in two weekends.

Susan Davis Shaw   Davisdane
52 East Street   (617) 826-3686
Hanover, MA 02339

CH. DINRO MCKENNA'S AGAINST ALL ODDS

```
                                    Ch. Castille's Gent of Mountdania
                        Ch. Pededane's Justinian
                                    Ch. Robmar's Fandi
            Beaucedane's Gent Jr. v Mt. Dania
                                    Ch. Castile's Gent of Mountdania
                        Ch. Castilles Cover Girl
                                    Ch. Castiles Buttercup v. Windfall
Ch. Dinro McKenna's Against All Odds
                                    Ch. Sunridge's Rag Time Cowboy Joe
                        Ch. Misty Valley's Andromeda
                                    Rockbridge's September Inga
            Ch. Dinro Desiree McKenna
                                    Ch. Dinro Diplomat
                        Dinro Yum Yum
                                    Murlo Olivia
```

We have been fortunate to have owned and bred over 35 champions the past 26 years. We have bred under the Sounda prefix since 1969 and under the Dinro prefix since 1978 after the untimely death of the late Rose Roberts, the original owner of Dinro Bloodline founded in 1935. To answer a most frequently asked question, we reserve the Dinro prefix for our Fawns and Brindles and the Sounda prefix for our Harlequins and Blacks. One of our proudest accomplishments is the "Brother Dog"- AKA Am. P. R., S. American, Ch. of the Americas, Multiple BISS Ch. Dinro McKenna's Against All Odds, bred by Carol Ann McKenna and Robert E. Layne. In addition to being a companion and visitation dog, combined with the expert handling of Edward Lyons Jr., this team successfully became the Number One Dane in the country for 1991. This winning team's record clearly speaks for itself.

Robert E. Layne and Louis G. Bond
P.O. Box 261
Millbury, MA 01527

Dinro Sounda
GREAT DANES

Dinro Sounda
(508) 865-2828
FAX (508) 865-3738

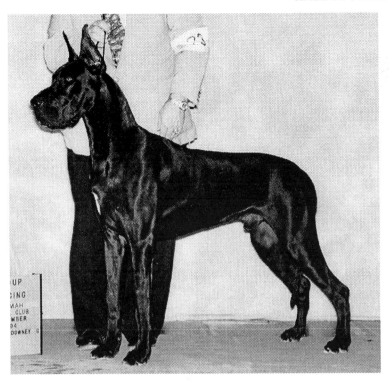

CH. REANNS SPELLBINDER

```
                                    Ch. Reann's Rated R
                        Ch. Reanns Joe Cool, CD
                                    Sterling Silouhette of Reanns
            Reann's Soul Seeker
                                    Ch. Reann's Dark Side of Sounda
                        Sounda's Dark Mystery V Reann
                                    Diana-Link's Visa V Sounda
Ch.   Reanns Spellbinder
                                    Ch. Hauerdane's War Bonnet
                        Reann's Royal Heir
                                    Ch. Reann's Happy Hooke
            Maridaz Efbe's Maggie's Return
                                    Ch. Tyler Lovett of Falconroc
                        Maridaz Efbe's Heritage
                                    Efbe's Blue Morning of Maridaz
```

This young dog, known as Clipper, finished his championship on two consecutive weekends in July 1994. He epitomizes the best traits of the breed, friendly and outgoing, yet a true "gentle giant." Bred and co-owned by Anita Langevin, GREAT DANE CLUB OF AMERICA'S 1994 BREEDER OF THE YEAR, he now calls Charma Danes his home. His handler and friend, Eddie Lyons, finished him and took him on his specials career.

Owners:
Chuck and Willie Crawford
Charma Danes
(770) 253-7277

Co-Owner:
Anita Langevin
Reanns Danes

WACCABUC'S DUST OF THE PHOENIX
CH. WACCABUC'S DIFFERENT DRUMMER
JAPANESE CH. WACCABUC'S DREAM OF GENIE

```
                              Ch. Rojon's the Hustler
                    Ch. Windane's Zephyr
                              Windane's April Storm, CD
          Ch. Shannon's Tycho Brahe
                              Ch. Von Riesenhof's the Boss
                    Piper's Ragalia V. Earl-Mar
                              Ch. Earl-Mar's Sandpiper
Waccabuc's  D  Litter
                              Ch. Gen-Ton's Sulton of Stonehouse
                    Cedardane's Cathian Suleiman
                              Ch. Cedardane's Roman Catherine P
          Waccabuc's Blanket Pardon
                              Devrok's Quo Titan Sabak, CD
                    Waccabuc's Aurora Borealis
                              Cedardane's Cathian Valideh, CD
```

Waccabuc Great Danes strives to breed functional, versatile, long-lived Danes. The functional Dane is sound in mind and body, capable of any endeavor for which he or she is trained. Waccabuc bred Danes have achieved AKC titles in conformation, obedience, and tracking and have been involved in other activities such as therapy work, Freestyle Heeling, Canine Good Citizen and Lure Coursing. Waccabuc Great Danes are excellent companions, many of whom have lived well past ten years of age.

Betty and Bill Lewis
17 Danbury Circle
Amherst, NH 03031

WACCABUC
(603) 673-DANE

BISS, AM/CAN CH. PAQUESTONE'S REBEL OF PAGE, CAN TD, CD
(born June 5, 1991)

```
                                      VonRaseac's French Gigalo
                      Am Ch. VonRaseac's French Dandy
                                      Hillview's Chantilly
              Am Ch. R-D Viking Dane's Shotgun
                                      Am Ch. Stockdale's Corporate Dividend
                      Am Ch. Viking Dane's Tyra V Stockdale
                                      Viking's Gypsy V Stockdale
BISS Am/Can Ch. Paquestone's Rebel of Page, Can TD, CD
                                      Am Ch. Barnette's Brave Warrior
                      BISS Am/Can Ch. Paquestone's Der Gut Kamerod
                                      Legend Rock's Burlesque
              Can Ch. Paquestone's Page of Wisdom
                                      Am Ch. Barnette's Zebra
                      Am/Can Ch. Paquestone's Java
                                      Can Ch. Paquestone's Go-Rilla-Go
```

Since 1980, "Paquestone Great Danes" has produced or co-bred at least thirty Canadian and twenty American Champions. We breed only one or two litters per year. Many of our dogs have obedience and tracking titles. I am proud to have bred one of the few Danes to receive an American Agility title. Over the years we have had several bitches and dogs listed as top producers for the breed in the United States. Our Danes are always bred with the greatest care to produce intelligent dogs that are sound in mind and body. I've always felt fortunate to have been able to successfully place "Paquestone Great Danes" with wonderful and caring people.

Raymond R. Goldstone
1711 Pacific Highway RR #3
Surrey, B.C., Canada   V4P1M6

Paquestone Great Danes
(604) 541-0445

CH. LAUREL SPRINGS LETHAL WEAPON

Ch. Sandale's What A Guy
Ch. Von Shrado's I'm A Knock Out
Ch. Von Shrado's Easter bonnet
Ch. Nightwind's Time Traveler
Ch. Regene Brigadier V Jonathie
Ch. Nightwind's Sheer Elegance
Cherryhill's Canadian Mist
Ch. Laurel Springs Lethal Weapon
Ch. Deer Run's Top Gun
Goldndanes Overthtop Deerun
Deer Run's Voodoo of Oak Hill
Aspen of Laurel Springs Farm
Deer Run's Adrian Von Odin
Golden Danes Summer Breeze
Shadams Nadine of Pappy Jack

In the Dane world, Laurel Springs Kennel in Mount Holly, Virginia, is a young kennel. It has two homebred champions and many other Great Danes with points. We began with our Deer Run bitch being bred to Ch. Nightwinds Time Traveler. Out of that stock Laurel Springs Champions began and continue. Laurel Springs Lethal Weapon, "Tank," was our first champion. He was a beautiful red brindle with a gentle temperament, outstanding movement, and a lot of personality. He always carried his teddy bear and curled up with it each night. He won Best of Breeds over top twenty dogs in the country. Wherever he went he drew a crowd of admirers. Laurel Springs Piece d'Art is our second homebred champion owned by Mary Ann and Patrick Dogan. He continues to reflect the temperament, conformation and breed type that we are striving for. Tank has sired a lovely young brindle male, Laurel Springs Harley Super Glide, owned by Stephanie Gallups, making his debut and finishing in the 1996 show season. My philosophy on breeding is simple. Breed for temperament, and movement, and always look to the future.

William and Laurie Crossman
P.O. Box 220
Mount Holly, VA 22524-0220

Laurel Springs Danes
(804) 472-3513

AM/CAN CH. SHADY LANE'S PIECE OF THE ROCK

```
                              Donnadane's Guy of Jaylor
                      Excalibur's Show Em the Duke
                              Gretchen Sapphira MGM
              Winston of Posom Holow
                              Gentleman of Cedar Hill
                      Zucker Kindlein
                              Brennan's Dazzling Delilah
      Am/Can ch. Shady Lane's Piece of the Rock
                              Ch. Sandale What A Guy
                      Ch. Woodcliff's Charles Sandale
                              Ch. Woodcliff's Gentle Nancy
              Woodcliff's Pride 'N' Joy
                              Ch. Woodcliff's Bold Bracken
                      Velikon's Radiant Raquel
                              Colvin's Star Ialeya Velikon
```

"Bam-Bam" began his career with a Best in Sweepstakes at the GDC of Raritan Valley Specialty, at nine months of age. He quickly added another Best in Sweeps as a junior dog and sailed to both his American and Canadian Championships before two years of age, taking Best of Breeds and group placements along the way. He was bred by Joyce and Marvin Davis, Shady Lane Danes, and stems from Peg and Dick Nelson's Woodcliff Kennels. This young dog exemplifies the quality heritage from hence he came. He is producing sound, beautiful, typey, sweet tempered puppies. We look forward to the future with him!

Sunrise
Melissa & William C. Dreyer, Jr.
81 Crease Rd
Budd Lake, NJ 07828
(201) 691-9413

Shady Lane
Joyce & Marvin Davis
2702 Sunnyside Blvd
Greenville, NC 27834
(919) 752-7657

CH. JERDAN'S BENCHMARK V CARMA QUE

```
                              Ch. Dagon's In A Flash
                    Ch. Shadam's Gregory
                              Ch. Shadam's Brooke
          Ch. Jerdan's Top Priority
                              Willow Lakes Augustus
                    Ch. Jerdan's Miss Emma
                              Jerdan's Cara Mia Michaeldane
Ch. Jerdan's Benchmark V Carma Que
                              Ch. Dagon's in a Flash
                    Ch. Shadam's Gideon
                              Ch. Shadam's Brooke
          Shadam's Jamie Lee
                              Ch. Shadam's Benson
                    Shadam's Merry Miss V Jaco
                              Windane's Merry Meagan
```

Benchmark Great Danes is owned by Kevin and Charlotte Cavell of Baton Rouge, Louisiana, and is committed to producing sound Great Danes that are not only excellent in conformation but are also excellent in temperament. The Cavells purchased their first Great Dane as a family companion, but then became interested in obedience and began competing in that sport. Interest in exhibiting in the conformation ring soon followed and their fawn dog, Ben, has done quite a bit of winning in that area beginning with his prestigious Award of Merit win at the 1994 Great Dane Club of America National Specialty Show. Ben is co-owned by Dr. Jose Ribo and was bred by Marsha and Brenda Schaublin, all of Ohio. (Photo by John Bridges, 1995)

Kevin and Charlotte Cavell
13144 Country Manor Ave.
Baton Rouge, LA 70816

Benchmark Great Danes
(504) 751-5913

CH. LEATRICK'S KISS OF FIRE

Riverwood's Ringtop Jagla
Ch. Heritage's Beta Von Riverwood
Ch. Heritage's Chardonnay
BISS Ch. Patchwork's Ashley Wilkes
Ch. Koenigdane's Prince Perseus
BISS Ch. Suschen's Spirit of Christmas
Suschen's Ein Kopie Der Lilli
Ch. Leatrick's Kiss of Fire
Ch. BMW Ruffian
BIS Ch. BMW Bull Lea
Ch. BMW Fantasia
Michaeldanes Dagon's Cameo
GMJ's The Condour
GMJ's The Lady Celeste
Dean's First Lady

"Haley" is one of two champions out of Leatrick Great Dane's foundation bitch, Michaeldane Dagon's Cameo. Her brother, Ch. Leatrick's Grand Illusion, is the 1991 National Futurity winner. Leatrick's continues to produce outstanding Harlequin and Boston puppies for conformation, obedience, and companions.

Breeder and Co-Owner:
Tim & Lori Keefe
Owner:
Clay Stephenson
Eddie Sturgal
Westside Danes
Leatrick Great Danes
9061 Tiber St
Bay St. Louis, MS 39520
(610) 467-4985

CH. RIKA WILDWIND BLACK ICE

O'Lorcain's Townleigh V. Hauer
Ch. Hauerdane's War Bonnet
Rysco's Million Dollar Baby
Ch. Wildwind Rampage V. Hillhaus
Ch. Rory Von Sligo of Wildwind
Glory B Von Sligo
Ch. Cory Von Sligo of Wildwind
Ch. Rika Wildwind Black Ice
Ch. Longo's Chief Joseph
Ch. Longo's Primo D'Aquino
Ch. Aquino's Oso Perla Negra
Ch. Penedane's Wages of Sin Etal
Ch. Sheenwater Gamble On Me
Ch. Penedane's Notorious Lady
Ch. Saltwater's Doubloon

Wildwind Great Danes began in 1967 with the acquisition of Doria Von Riverwood Ranch, a black bitch out of black and fawn breeding. We were fortunate to begin with a quality Dane who also produced well. We've bred very few litters over the years (8) and are the breeders of 16 champions, to the best of my recollection, with numerous champions out of our stud dogs as well. I became an AKC approved judge for Great Danes in 1992 which I throughly enjoy. We live with only one Great Dane at the moment, Ch. Rika Wildwind Black Ice, a product of frozen sperm, our first in that department.

Jill and Terry Ferrera
9200 Encino Ave
Northridge, CA 91325

Wildwind Great Danes
(818) 993-8948
FAX (818) 993-8944

BIS, BISS CH. AMHERST-HARLWOOD BUBBA RONDO

Ch. BMW Bull Lea

Ruths Rambo N'Co

GMJ's The New Yorker And Co

Ch. Riverwood's Rondo

Ch. BMW Bull Lea

Riverwood's Ringtop Nevey

Ringtop's Edelweiss Von DMS

BIS, BISS, Ch. Amherst-Harlwood Bubba Rondo

BMW Winston Churchill

Ch. Chauffeured's Dr. Levy J.R.

Chauffeured's Coalette

Dan-Mar's Jazmin Potpourri

Ruths Rambo N'Co

Dan-Mar's Jazmin V Riverwood

Riverwood's Snowdrift

The Number One Great Dane for 1996, Bubba has had a very distinguished show career. He ranked among the top twenty Great Danes in the country for three consecutive years. But undoubtedly his greatest contribution to the breed will be his offspring. He has consistently produced get renowned for their type, soundness,   movement and attitude. Bubba won Top Stud Dog at the GDCA National Specialty   in 1996. He was the Top Producer for 1995 — the first time a Harlequin ever won   this distinction — and he is a leading contender for repeating the honor in 1996.   Bubba's handler is Jinny Rojas.

Betty Lou Wood
106 Gilder Creek Drive
Simpsonville, SC 29681

Harlwood Danes
(864) 963-6019

CH. VALI HI'S FLASH BLACK

```
                              Ch. Honey Lane's Rave Review
                    Ch. Dagon's in a Flash
                              BIS Ch. Dagon's I'm Pixie
            Ch. Fairoaks Razoredge Hayeaker
                              Ch. Darrdane's Opening Bid
                    Ch. Fairoaks Magon V Falconroc
  Ch. Vali Hi's Flash Black
                              Ch. Shannon's Tycho Brahe
                    BIS Ch. Corinth's I Am Abel V Hydane
                              Ch. Hydane's Femme Fatale
            Karadane's Ebony Charade
                              Ch. Shadowbrook's Bask
                    Karadane's Bask Silhouette
                              Emmen's Black Satin
```

"Flashy" completed her Am. championship with 4 majors and represents the breeding program established in 1967 by Vali Hi Great Danes, focusing primarily on Black, Fawn and Black/Fawn breeding programs. Flashy is a great great granddaughter of Ch. Charlemagne Du Lac, bred by Vali Hi and owned by Pat and Howard Bates. Charlemagne or "Charlie" (as his many fans knew him) is pictured in the Dog Shows chapter of this book. Charlie is prominently found in the pedigrees of the top winning Black Danes in the U.S., such as Ch. Longo's Chief Joseph and Ch. Longo's Sweettalk V. Michaeldane, both of which achieved the status of number 1 Great Dane in the U.S. during their careers.

Jeanette & Jim Pickett
4301 Appaloosa Dr
Myrtle Beach, SC 29577

Vali Hi Great Danes
(803) 236-4980
FAX (803) 236-2954
e-mail NATURFARM@AOL.COM

printed for each show, listing each dog entered, its name, owner, breeder and age. Dogs will show first. Puppy dogs, Novice dogs, Bred by Exhibitor dogs (those whose breeders are actually showing them), American Bred dogs (open to any dog bred in the United States), and Open dogs. In some shows, the open class may be divided into classes for different colors. The first place winners from each class will go back into the ring to pick Winners Dog. Then the bitches show, through the same classes, and the first place winners will return for Winners Bitch. Only the top dog and bitch will win points; all other dogs and bitches will go home empty handed!

For that reason, owners often hire handlers. These professionals know how to present a dog to its best advantage, and they know the judges and what certain judges are looking for in a dog. Sometimes, a dog will travel with the handler to the show and the owner does not attend at all. If your breeder sold you your dog with a contract which says he must be shown, you may be required to send the dog with a handler in order to get him "finished," that is, to earn his championship. Sometimes owners will show their own dogs, and that is referred to as "owner handled." You may see that term in our Hall of Fame section.

Ch. Charlemagne Du Lac is in the pedigree of many of the top winning Black Danes of recent years.

Great Danes are highly competitive. They are ranked thirty-three in number of dogs registered each year in the AKC, but they are quite frequently in the top ten for entries at any given show. There are a *lot* of people who are actively showing their Great Danes, and it is considered a very competitive breed because of the high number of entries. Beagles, for example, register over three times as many dogs each year as Great Danes, yet it takes only four or six Beagles to make a major instead of twenty or thirty Great Danes. For that reason, it is difficult for a novice handler to win with a Great Dane. If you are new to dog showing, it is probably wise to consider hiring a handler until you learn about dog shows and how to show your dog to his best advantage.

Once a dog has earned his title, he will show only in the "Best of Breed" (BOB) class. Champions, and the Winner's Dog and Winner's Bitch for the day, will return to the ring to select the "Best of Breed." If the Best of Breed is a dog, a bitch will be chosen as "Best of Opposite Sex." If the Best of Breed is a bitch, a dog will be named Best of Opposite Sex. Only the Best of Breed will return to the group ring at the end of the day to compete in the "Group."

All breeds are divided into one of seven Groups: Sporting, Non-Sporting, Herding, Working, Terriers, Toys and Hounds. There are about fifteen to twenty breeds in each group. Great Danes are in the Working Group. The winner of each group will return to the Best in Show ring where the final seven dogs compete to be named the Best in the Show. Many of you have watched parts of the Group judging or Best in Show judging from Madison Square Garden on cable television. Other famous local shows are sometimes broadcast.

In the early days of showing, in the 1930s, all champions were in the Open Class, and "Specials Only" meant your dog was for sale or on exhibition. Almost all shows were benched, with dogs tethered on chains. There were raised platforms in the middle of the ring which the udges used to compare exhibits, and the winner was always placed "On the Block." Most of the exhibitors were people of wealth and social position, and owners seldom showed their own dogs.

Westminster was a three-day affair offering benching. Colored cards in place of ribbons were displayed on the back of each dog's bench to help the public recognize the winners. Kennel men often spent the night on the benches with the dogs. Today there are only about a half a dozen bench shows left in the country, with the Westminister Kennel Club show in Madison Square Garden being the most famous.

Today, the average AKC show will have about 1,000 to 1,500 dogs entered. Some will have entries of 2,500 to 3,500. One show in Louisville, Kentucky, has reached 5,000 entries!

There is a lot of excitement at a show, and usually ten to twenty-five rings are being judged at once. If you do not have the judging schedule ahead of time and wish to be sure to see a certain breed, be sure to arrive as early as 8:30 in the morning.While some shows do not begin until 9:00, some shows start as early as 8:00. Each breed is judged at a certain pre-scheduled time in a specific ring. A judging schedule is available ahead of time to exhibitors and generally arrives in the mail about three to four days before the show. If you arrive too late, you may find that the breed you are interested in has already been judged early in the morning, and only the Best of Breed dog is still on the grounds. Or, the dogs may be back at their vans and cars, scattered across a large parking lot and almost impossible to find. We have very few classic Bench Shows left in this country, so dogs are not on exhibit all day. They are brought up from their cars and vans, shown, and returned to rest until their owners are ready to go home.

HOW TO KNOW A STAR

Dog showing is a subjective sport. People who show, talk about the fine points of conformation. But almost everyone agrees that "quality" and "balance" are just as important as any single asset. "Balance" refers to the way the front and rear of a dog go together, the way a dog moves and the proportions of the dog, and how they all fit together. But there is another factor in a top winning dog. It is elusive, and cannot truly be defined, but it is called "presence." One breeder describes a retired show dog at eight years of age. "He came into a large room, stood there and looked at you. Everything else in the room faded away. I have never seen a photograph that does him justice. The memory of him that day is implanted in my mind forever." A show dog with presence can sometimes have a few faults. He may not be as perfect as another dog, but he has a style, a quality that, like an actor or a model, sets him apart. He is charismatic, and a judge is attracted to him.

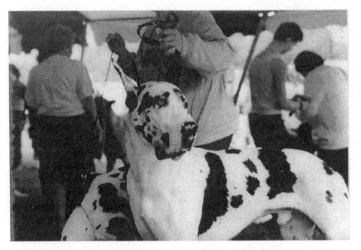

Under the tent at a typical show is a scene of noise and confusion. Great Danes generally adapt easily to the crowds of people and other dogs.

Some dogs are called "Package Dogs." They are nice in a number of ways. They may have a good head, though not as good as some other entries. But they are good movers and have sound conformation, balance and presence. They have no large faults, so they go together in a well balanced package, and they are strong in a number of ways. This combination is what makes a truly great show dog.

But remember, there is no such thing as a perfect dog, or one which wins all the time. The top winning dog at Madison Square Garden, or at the Nationals, may fail to get a ribbon the next day under a different judge. Opinions of judges will be different depending on their personal experiences and beliefs. The stronger the competition is between good dogs, the more disagreements there are because the finer points of judging require personal evaluation. There are no numerical standards. One characteristic may be listed as a fault, but so might another on a different dog and there is nothing to say which is better or which is worse. A judge may be looking at one dog with a good neck and head, but a bad tailset, while another has a wonderful topline, but a common head. These are values which must be subjectively weighed by a judge. This is a beauty contest. What a judge ultimately points at (selects as his winner) depends on his personal beliefs of which is a more serious fault, and what good points he values. Perhaps he will go with a dog which has no faults, but no outstanding features either. What is often taken as "crooked" judging is simply a matter of personal values on the part of the judge which may differ from those of the spectator or exhibitor. Remember, we do not ask a judge to tell us what he thinks is a perfect Great Dane. We ask him his opinion in picking the best of what is in front of him that day. Like people, dogs may have good and bad days where they are more or less interested in showing. How well a dog *likes* to show is an important element, and gives him the "presence" he needs to be a winner.

There are no hard and fast rules determining what is a show dog. Any dog with full AKC registration can be a show dog by paying the entry fee, and if it has no disqualifying faults, it will be allowed to compete to the extent of completing its class. Some dogs are so average that they will consistently place under almost all judges, even in strong competition, but they will never win, for although they have no faults, they have no great assets either. Others will win one day under a judge who appreciates their good qualities, and lose another day under a judge who puts emphasis on an area where they are weak. These dogs have an up and down career but probably will still finish their championship before the dog with no great faults, but no great assets.

Keep this in mind when you are buying a show dog, and keep it in mind when you are beginning to show. And remember what one of our breeders says: "A good judge is one who puts up my dog, a bad judge puts up someone else's dog, and a terrible judge puts up my worst enemy's dog!" Dog showing is a competitive sport. Over the years, exhibitors learn to appreciate certain things in a dog and dislike others. Breeders develop their own style within their kennel, and dogs which are not of that style are "inferior" in their minds. But they are not the judge. The judge may agree with them one day and disagree with them another day. All of this is to say that if you buy a dog, one of the worst things you can do is take it to a show and ask all the other exhibitors what they think of it. The opinions you get back are more likely to reflect the feelings of the individual exhibitor toward the style, and even the breeder of the dog, than an absolute evaluation of the dog. The complexity of dog showing is one of the things that interests and fascinates people in the sport, and keeps them dedicated in time and money for many years.

Novice owners frequently take a young dog to a show, and when it does not win the first time or two, they begin to drag it around to other breeders and judges and inquire about its faults. This is very counterproductive, because all it does is call everyone's attention to the negative parts of the dog, so that even when he does develop and would normally begin to win, everyone remembers the faults that have been pointed out early in the dog's career. Also, remember it is easier for people to make negative comments about a potential competitor than it is to recognize the good qualities and point out how to best present the strengths. Questioning another breeder is like asking a competing coach how to improve another team! If you have not bought a pup from the local breeders, they may resent the fact that they were overlooked when you went outside the area. Even if you bought your dog from a local breeder, other breeders in the area may comment on the dog (either in a negative or positive way) with more of an eye to how much they like the person who sold you the dog than on how nice the dog really is. More than one dog has been sent back to a breeder because the novice owner did not feel it was "show quality," and the breeder has finished it easily.

If you are interested in showing, go to a show and see how your dog does in competition. If he wins, enjoy your success. If he loses several shows, consider that he may not be developed enough (if he is still immature). Sometimes a dog which cannot win as a puppy or young adult will mature into a fine show dog; he simply needed time to develop. Sometimes a judge will talk to you if you wait until after his assignment is over, though he is not required to do so and some of them do not like talking to exhibitors or novice owners. Another reason your dog may be losing is that the you might not be able to show him to his best advantage. Find a professional handler, and ask him or her about showing, or at least evaluating your dog. These people handle a number of different breeds from a wide variety of breeders. They know, overall, what a quality dog is and what it takes to get a dog finished. They are a more objective source of information than competing breeders or exhibitors.

Good breeders will not guarantee that a puppy will be a great show dog. They will sell a pup based on pedigree and what other, older siblings have done in the ring, and how the pup looks compared to his parents and other litters from the same bloodline. The longer a breeder has bred and shown, the better idea he or she will have of the *potential* a pup has. But there are seldom guarantees because there are so many variables. The area of the country a dog shows in will make a difference in how fast he finishes. Who handles him and how well he is conditioned

and presented will make a difference. How much the dog *enjoys* showing will make a difference. Even experiences he has in the ring during his first few months of showing will make a difference.

NEVER EXPECT ANYONE TO GUARANTEE THAT A PUPPY WILL BE A GROUP PLACING DOG. Group placings are dependent on many different things, from the competition that day to the early care a dog has received. Many people who want a group placing dog simply buy an older dog who already has started his show career and done well. Often handlers will find a dog they think has great promise and approach an owner about purchasing it. Sometimes, people who want a group placing dog will simply offer to "back" a dog which is already being shown and winning. This means that the "backer" puts his or her name on the dog and receives the fame for the dog's wins, and in return pays the bills to a greater or lesser extent, depending on the arrangement. Several Westminster winners have been "owned" by backers who never bred or owned another dog of that breed, and who have no kennel and no intention of ever breeding. When the dog was finished showing, he simply went back to the original owner who used him or her for breeding purposes and gave the dog a home for the rest of its life.

No mention of Great Danes in the show ring would be complete without mention of Lina Basquette. This flamboyant woman, a half-sister to Marge Champion of the famous dancing team Marge and Gower Champion, was a silent movie star in her younger years. She was the first pupil to enroll in Universal's school for movie children. Her career included being a poster girl for war bond promotion during the First World War and being a Ziegfeld Follies star. Her seven husbands, beginning with Sam Warner in 1925, and well known lovers, including the boxer Jack Demsey and organized crime boss Johnny Roselli among many others of equal notoriety, set the tone for her life. She made numerous pictures with popular co-stars of the era such as Hoot Gibson, Ward Bond, Tom Keene, Ken Maynard and Buck Jones.

As judge of the Westchester KC show in 1991, Lina took the lead of the dog she had just awarded Best of Breed and showed off her style once again. At 84 years old she still loved dogs and loved putting on a show for the crowd.

For much of her life, Lina was involved in breeding, showing and handling Great Danes. Her kennel Honey Hollow produced many great dogs. In the show ring she was a well known breeder, a dramatic and exciting exhibitor and, finally, a sought after judge. In 1983 she won the Working Group with a Great Dane at Westminister — something which has seldom been done. When she passed away in 1995, well into her eighties, the dog show world lost a colorful and fascinating figure.

OBEDIENCE

Working dogs (those whose career is based on what they can do, not how they look, such as obedience dogs) can continue to show for many years. They get better with age, often understanding what is expected better than they did when they were young. If the owner is careful to make the work fun for the dog, a dog who competes in the working division can continue to show for many years after he retires from the conformation ring.

Dogs with working titles earn their titles for life through a series of performances where they earn a qualifying score, that is, a score which is high enough to earn them a "leg" on their title. Most performance competition is done on a point system, and more than one dog a day can earn points toward his title. If he performs well, he will be rewarded. Performance or working titles *follow* the registered name of the dog, and once earned, are printed each time the name of the dog is written.

Obedience is an event at most dog shows. Unlike conformation showing, where no special training is needed to start showing a young dog, obedience dogs are required to show off-lead and through a specific set of exercises. Judging is very precise. Scoring is done by subtracting points for faults such as failing to sit square, to return fully, or to stay in step on the heel exercise. Conformation dogs do not need to sit — in fact they should **not** sit while in the ring. Obedience dogs are required to sit when the handler stops walking and when a command is given throughout the exercise program. Conformation classes and obedience classes are held at the same time, so it is very difficult, especially for a young dog and a novice handler, to adapt to the different types of showing, and to work with the conflicting schedules which often develop.

Obedience dogs need to have reached a level of training so that they can go through precise movements on the command of their handlers, including heel, sit, stay and down. One of the biggest problems for a Great Dane is the jumping. Because of their size, they are required to jump thirty inches high or more. One breeder suggests not jumping dogs more than eighteen inches when training indoors and to restrict the number of times you ask them to jump, because stress injuries are always a possibility.

An obedience dog must be by nature intelligent and willing to please. Great Danes can compete well, especially if the handler takes care to make it fun for them. You will notice that several of the dogs in the Hall of Fame have obedience titles.

One of our breeders who has finished several obedience dogs, says that a Great Dane will work well, but they are of a totally different temperament than, say, an Australian Shepherd or a Golden Retriever. Those breeds want to please their owner, and will repeat the task over and over. A Great Dane will be happy to work with you, but will want to know the reason why he is doing something; he wants to know how long it will last and what the goal is. And when he has done it, he feels the task is completed and does not see a reason to do it again and again. So, working for the perfection needed for obedience work (such as sitting an inch closer and facing directly ahead instead of at an angle) can create a very bored dog who then gives up. After that point he only pays attention with half his mind and he knows he can do the task with a minimum amount of effort. This in turn leads to a deteriorating performance. Both partners must pay attention and be happy in order to have a good performance. If the handler is having fun, the dog will have fun and pay attention. If the work is approached as an exacting exercise to be practiced, the dog will quickly lose attention and attitude. One obedience expert feels that people tend to drill Great Danes too much, relying on the type of practice needed for other breeds. New owners who attend obedience classes aimed at other breeds or who read books on the subject put too much importance on repetition and not enough emphasis on making the dog happy, interested and challenged by the work at hand.

Another breeder agrees that keeping a Dane interested is the biggest problem, and that the secret to a good obedience dog was to convince him that the exercises you are training him to do are the best game in town. If it is fun and continues to be fun, he will do it. Another breeder suggests that she finds herself being part trainer, part cheerleader and part treat dispenser when she trains her obedience dogs.

The biggest pitfalls for them are heeling and sitting with precision. The fraction of an inch between sloppy heeling and sitting and a precise sit or heel which will earn a top score just does not seem to be important to them.

Dogs begin with the Novice class. A and B divisions relate to the handler. "A" dogs are handled by their owners, and only one dog may be shown in the class. The "B" division allows a dog to be handled by a professional handler or trainer. Several dogs may be handled by the same owner or handler in the same class in the "B" division.

There are six exercises which score points: Heel on Leash, Stand for Examination, Heel Free, Recall, Long Sit and Long Down, with a possible total of 200. All but the Heel on Leash must be done off-lead, and a dog must score at least 50% of the available points in each exercise *and* have a total score of 170 or higher in three obedience trials (with at least six dogs in competition) to earn a C.D. (Companion Dog) title. Once this is earned, the dog moves up to the next level.

The second level has seven exercises. Each must be precisely executed. They are: Heel Free, Drop on Recall, Retrieve on Flat, Retrieve Over High Jump, Broad Jump, Long Sit and Long Down. Three qualifying scores at three different shows are needed to earn the title of C.D.X. (Companion Dog Excellent). Dogs may then move up to earn a U.D. (Utility Dog) title. This is the highest title an obedience dog can earn. The seven exercises include scent discrimination, hand signals, and both broad and high jumps.

Obedience classes mix all breeds together, though each dog is scored against a perfect performance, not against the other dogs in competition that day. Thus every dog competing that day could theoretically qualify, or no dog that day could qualify, depending on the performances of each dog.

Almost any show has classes for obedience. They are usually held in a ring apart from the conformation showing. If you are interested in showing your dog in obedience, begin with a local obedience class. Be prepared to work

with him on a daily basis for several months before you attempt to show. You may want to start showing at a local "match show." These are practice shows for both conformation and obedience. They offer no points toward a title, but they are usually small, with limited competition and no pressure and they are a good place to begin to learn the dog show game.

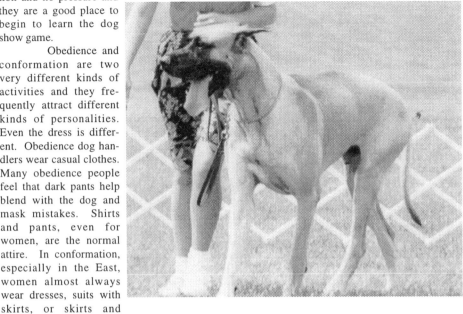

Obedience and conformation are two very different kinds of activities and they frequently attract different kinds of personalities. Even the dress is different. Obedience dog handlers wear casual clothes. Many obedience people feel that dark pants help blend with the dog and mask mistakes. Shirts and pants, even for women, are the normal attire. In conformation, especially in the East, women almost always wear dresses, suits with skirts, or skirts and blouses. Men wear sports coats and ties, except on very hot days, when the judge may indicate that the coat may be disregarded. Men are seldom seen without a tie, jeans are not appropriate, and women are almost never seen in pants. In California, and some other areas, golf shirts and pants are sometimes worn, though jeans and T-shirts are never considered appropriate.

AGILITY

Begun in 1977 in England, Agility is an obstacle course for dogs. It is fun, fast, and growing in popularity each year. Dogs go through a series of obstacles, over a bridge, on teeter totters, through tunnels and barrels, between poles, and over A-frames. Great Danes are sometimes too large to maneuver the obstacles, although they may like the variety of the work and enthusiastically enjoy what they can do in that area. While many of our breeders do not recommend agility for Danes, one or two breeders say they are beginning to work some of their dogs in agility and are getting good results. One of our breeders cautions that some of the obstacles are not safe for Danes, while others, such as the simple weaving poles, are not set for dogs of giant proportion. Be careful and use good judgment when introducing your Dane to agility and think about his safety before you send him over something which may be perfectly safe for an average size dog.

Dogs must be over six months old, and able to compete through obstacles off lead. Dogs compete against time over the obstacles and lose points for failing to complete an obstacle as described. Qualifying scores add toward titles, but high score dogs at an event are also recognized. Call your local kennel club for details of Agility Clubs in your area. Most kennel clubs have at least a few members who are interested or active in agility and new clubs are forming every year. Agility is one of the fastest growing new sports involving dogs and attracts people from all walks of life. Several of the major dog food companies have sponsored events, and in addition to competitions, there are many agility exhibitions at dog shows and other spectator events throughout the country each year.

For those who are very interested, there is a National Championship. A dog must qualify to compete, and for many years these finals have been held in Houston, Texas, in the

Astrodome. This competition has attracted dogs from all over the country and in almost all breeds.

AKC CANINE GOOD CITIZEN TEST AND TEMPERAMENT TESTING

Recently, the AKC has added the Canine Good Citizen test, recognizing the need for responsible dog ownership and the recognition of well trained pets. Most clubs put on a CGC test at least once a year. This test, which lasts most of a day, tests the dog's ability to do basic obedience, and his attitude in meeting new people and new situations. If he passes the test, he is awarded a CGC title. These tests are growing in popularity and more and more dogs are showing up with CGC attached to their names.

Temperament Testing is somewhat similar, though it is not done through AKC. These tests require a dog to meet friendly strangers, hostile strangers, neutral strangers, and a variety of situations. Again, the test will take up the better part of a day, but the title earned will stay with the dog for life. You will see a number of dogs in the Hall of Fame with CGC or TT at the end of their name indicating that they have entered and passed one of these competitions.

Great Danes are also good Therapy Dogs in spite of their size and several of them hold licensed therapy titles. They appear in nursing homes, sometimes dressed up for the occasion, and bring joy and comfort to the residents. These gentle giants are great favorites and enjoy meeting strangers and the attention. They are large and rugged, so an unsteady hand does not bother them, but they can brighten the day of a person to whom the touch of a dog brings back warm memories of companions long since passed away.

CARE OF THE GREAT DANE

*G*reat Danes require very little grooming. A bath from time to time will keep the dog clean, and a brushing with a hound brush or natural bristle mitt will keep the coat shiny. They do not take long to dry — a brisk rub with a towel is enough to nearly dry them completely. They have very little doggie odor and don't shed heavily. In many cases, they can simply be wiped down with a wet cloth to get off dirt and mud after a romp in a spring mud puddle! During times of the year when they shed, a hand-held vacuum will serve to take up the loose hair and keep it off your sofa. A point of concern may be when Black dogs sometimes appear to have small white specks all over the coat. Breeders report getting calls from new owners who said their dogs had a variety of skin problems. Most black dogs, in most breeds, will have this condition from time to time. Actually, all dogs get the condition; but it simply is not easy to see on light colored dogs. Dead skin cells, which are replaced by new cells in dogs — and in humans — on a regular basis are the cause, and it is a perfectly natural occurrence. The white specks are most noticeable right after a bath, when the massage motion of shampooing has knocked loose a number of these dead cells. The condition will not hurt the dog, and does not mean there is a skin problem. But if it bothers you to look at the white spots, put mouthwash in a spray bottle and mist the dog. They will disappear immediately, as the mouthwash dissolves the cells. This is an old trick used by show breeders for years to present the coat in the best possible light when exhibiting their animals.

Many coat problems are related to fleas. If your dog has hair loss or raw spots begin with flea treatment, especially if you are in a flea area or it is flea season. (See more about fleas in the chapter on health.)

Regular veterinarian care is essential to any dog. Shots and worming are a part of your puppy's life and a yearly necessity after he is a year old. (Again, more about that in the health chapter.)

EAR CROPPING

Ear cropping dates back to the time when the Great Dane was used as a hunting dog. A short crop helped reduce injuries by removing a natural target for the dog's prey. A short working crop is very easy to care for, since the natural muscle of the ear will cause a short cropped ear to stand with almost no encouragement. Over the years, however, ear cropping has become longer and more elegant to accentuate the neck and head of the dog. Crops may vary some from breeder to breeder and from one area of the country to another, with ears being somewhat taller and narrower in California than on the East Coast.

 "Pocketing"  Bases Bending  Correct Carriage

Ear care of a pup can be tedious. Your pup may arrive in racks, foam cones or even with his ears taped to Dixie cups. Taping and support may be needed for weeks or even months, depending on the age of the pup and the condition of the ear. How the ear is cut, the strength and thickness of the ear leather and the location of the ear on the head are all factors in how long it takes for the ears to stand and how much care is needed. Young pups will need to have their ears kept very clean to prevent infection and tape will need to be replaced weekly, more frequently if there is a lot of discharge from the crop. *It is very important that you make time for ear care.* Ears which are not cared for properly may not stand, or if they do, they may lean or sag. By the time the dog is grown, it is too late, and no amount of care will get them to stand properly. Ears can make or break the looks of a dog. Proper taping is as important as the initial cropping. Remember that although cropped ears are lovely and elegant, cropped ears which do not stand are not a pleasing sight.

After cropping the ear will need complete support. Within a few weeks, the solid support will be reduced to tape and some kind of a stiff liner. Many of our breeders use Dr. Scholl's "moleskin" used for human foot protection. When this self-adhesive product is cut in strips — about an inch in width and the length of the ear — it will give the support to help the ears stand.

Taping can be frustrating. Your breeder will probably give you instructions on ear care, including drawings. Our breeders have several tips for ear care. Use porous cloth tape, at least 1/2 inch wide, but one inch is better. With new hypo-allergenic tape, far fewer animals develop a reaction to the tape which years ago frequently produced infections and sores. (Although some drug stores carry this tape, you may have to seek out a medical supply store.) Tape does not stick as well to dog ears as you might expect, at least not if you want it to. Nothing is more frustrating than taking the time to tape ears, only to have them fall out by the next morning. Skin-Bond or Uro-Bond 500 glue or cement are brush-on silicon skin adhesives that help keep stays in place. Or, to make tape stickier, spray the tape with tractor starting fluid or other spray ether product. When you want the tape off, it will want to stay in place. Use adhesive removal liquid to get the tape off without pulling off the hair, skin or newly healed scabs. If your pup develops an odor about the ears, beware that infection has set in. Call your breeder for suggestions.

Even after the ears can support themselves, you may need to re-tape them now and again as the dog grows. Ears may stand for several days or even a week or more, then suddenly sag and fall. Re-tape them immediately and leave them for several days. Take the tape off and see if they will stand. Use common sense and don't panic. Sometimes even ears which have stood nicely will sag when the pup goes through the stress of teething. Be sure you talk to your breeder if you have any questions or problems. If you live close to the breeder, you will probably either take the pup back to the breeder or to the vet who did the cropping for follow-up ear care. This may entail several visits, and can continue for many months. If you do not live close, talk to your breeder for suggestions. You may need to search out a vet or someone in your area who feels confident in doing follow-up ear care.

In adult dogs, ears should be checked and cleaned. With a large open ear, the Great Dane does not have the kind of ear problems often found in drop-eared dogs. But if the ear has an odor, is red or painful to the touch, or if the dog rubs his ears or shakes his head or carries it cocked to one side, the ears are probably infected. Fungal infections may be a problem in humid climates. If odor or other indications of infection appear, consult your vet for medication. The periodic use of a few drops of ear wash will help prevent infections.

Also, ear mites may need treatment. Watch for black "dirt" in the ear canal. If your dog has fleas, he probably also has ear mites. These conditions can be easily cured with a little time and low cost treatment. There are several good over-the-counter ear mite treatments which can be used if the black "dirt" appears. There are also a number of companies making good, all natural ear cleaners which help prevent ear mites and fleas and which help keep the ears clean, preventing infection before it starts.

NAILS

If you hear your dog's nails clicking on the floor, or if they appear to be especially long, they should be cut back. Show breeders keep the nails of their dogs very short as this keeps the dog "up on his feet" and keeps pads from splaying out, especially as the dog grows and develops. Many of our breeders prefer to grind down nails rather than cut them. With Black dogs, or dogs with black nails, it is almost impossible to see how far out the quick (or inner pulp) grows. When the quick is cut it will bleed, sometimes profusely. Grinding is a little slower but the grinder creates enough heat to cauterize the quick and prevents bleeding as it shortens the nail. Dogs usually respond better to grinding than cutting. Begin to grind your puppy's nails early to get him used to it, and you will have less problem with his feet spreading out. By the time he is an adult, he will be used to the process and give you less trouble than if you wait until he is an adult before you try it for the first time. Count on doing nails about every three weeks.

TEETH

Another general care chore is brushing the teeth. Do not use human toothpaste as it is designed for people, who do not swallow it, while dogs frequently swallow the toothpaste. Baking soda is one of the best things for brushing your dog's teeth, and it will not hurt him if consumed. Because most breeders recommend feeding well soaked dog food (because of the threat of bloat), Danes will need their teeth cleaned on a regular basis. Talk to your breeder and/ or your vet for their recommendations and begin the process early in the life of your pup so he will get used to it.

SHOW GROOMING

Great Danes are easy to groom for the show ring. They are basically a wash and wear dog, needing only a good bath and brushing. Before showing, whiskers will be trimmed off, and the hair along the back of the pasterns, under the front area and along the ears and tail is usually trimmed to give a cleaner line. A Great Dane who has been living as a pet or playing in the yard can become a show dog in just a few minutes in terms of grooming.

SHELTER

The Great Dane is **NOT** a weather resistant dog. They do not tolerate extreme temperatures well. Since Great Danes like and need human contact, most of them are house dogs. They will play outside in bad weather and will even romp in the snow, but they need a warm, clean place to come in, dry off, and settle into. Don't leave him outside in winter without shelter to keep the wind away. Heat is another problem if temperatures become too high. In the summer, be sure that your dog has good shelter from direct sun, and bring him into a cooled building if the temperature rises above ninety degrees. It is better to assume that the Great Dane will be a house dog than to plan to keep him in a kennel or a doghouse, and **NEVER, NEVER** keep him chained. If you want an outdoor dog, don't buy a Great Dane.

FEEDING

Great Danes grow very fast. They will grow from around twenty pounds at two months old (which may be when you bring one home) to sixty to seventy-five pounds by the time they are four months old, and around one hundred pounds by six months of age. At one point in their lives, Great Danes are the fastest growing animal on earth. It is no wonder that growth problems are frequent. The chapter on health has set out many of these problems, but it is important to emphasize that proper nutrition is essential, not just important. During the first critical year to year and a half, there are a number of "stress periods."

Most breeders recommend adding Vitamin C to the diet. Before cropping, at least 250 mg are advisable morning and night, with 500 to 1,000 mg morning and night being necessary for most of the growth period. Breeders feel that vitamin C helps prevent hip dysplasia and other bone problems. Most breeders feel that a dog over two years old has no further need for the added vitamins.

A puppy should be fed three to four times a day when he is very young, gradually decreasing the feedings to two by the time he is six months old, and some breeders feel that continuing to feed a Great Dane two or three small meals of well soaked food even after he is an adult helps prevent bloat. None of our breeders recommend free feeding, where the food is left in front of the dog all day and he feeds at will. A puppy will eat almost as much as an adult dog, and considering the size, Great Danes do not eat as much as most people think. A Dane will consume little more than a Lab or Doberman even though he is considerably larger.

It is especially important not to let a puppy put on too much weight, as it is hard on hips, joints and future health. Most of our breeders feel that dog foods of especially high protein should be avoided. Often, new owners are anxious to do well for their pets and buy the highest priced dog food with the intent of getting the best quality for their dog. But protein levels which are in the high range, 26 to 32 percent, are too high for either the average adult or growing pups. High protein dog foods have been blamed for most of the growth problems in Great Danes. Foods with protein levels as low as 21 percent are recommended, which means that most puppy or growth dog foods will be too high in protein. To feed an excessively high protein food to a dog that is not working or showing hard, is like feeding an office worker the same diet a pro football player would eat! The accelerating rate of kidney and digestive problems in dogs has often been blamed on the increased use of extremely high protein dog foods. In cold weather, a dog which is outside needs more nutrition to keep up his body weight. But remember that Great Danes do not tolerate temperature extremes very well. Table scraps are firmly discouraged as they add too much protein to the diet. One breeder suggests feeding only table scraps of fruits and vegetables which, surprisingly, most dogs enjoy.

Table scraps can add to another problem in Great Danes — flatulence. Danes can have some of the worst gas problems you will ever encounter. One breeder talks about going to a show with three grown Danes in a van and having to open the windows, even though it was freezing outside, simply to be able to breathe fresh air! Some breeders suggest changing food brands—keeping in mind protein level limitations.

Some dog foods have more bulk than others. Before you can say how much food a dog should eat a day, you must know if it is a high bulk or a low volume dog food. The obvious advantage to the low volume dog foods is that they also produce less waste to clean up. High bulk dog foods are viewed by some breeders as being inferior because they contain filler. Others feel the bulk is good for the dog's digestive system.

Because Great Danes are very tall they should always be fed from an elevated food bowl. We have mentioned this in the chapter on bringing your dog home, but it is important to remember as part of daily care. Feed the dog at shoulder height to reduce digestive problems and back problems and to make him more comfortable. There are several types of feeders which elevate the food bowl. You can put the bowl on a chair or stool, but the problem is that as the dog eats and pushes against the bowl, he will frequently push the bowl off onto the floor. You can make a feeder by turning a large bucket upside down and cutting a hole the size of the food bowl in the bottom. Drop the food bowl into the hole in the bottom of the bucket. Or, there are a number of companies which sell pre-made food stands. These are easy to keep clean, sometimes adjustable and nice looking. Some stands have built-in storage for food, brushes or other dog supplies.

If your dog goes off his feed, take his temperature immediately. A dog's normal temperature is 100 to 102 degrees, and it is helpful to take your dog's temperature from time to time so you can get a baseline on what his temperature is under normal circumstances. Inflamed and enlarged tonsils are one of the most common causes of an elevated temperature. The tonsils can often be seen by simply opening the dog's mouth and looking down the throat.

Some breeders recommend removing the tonsils if infections become frequent.

Bloat is always a problem. Since this condition occurs suddenly and is life-threatening (see the discussion in the health chapter), you should keep a watchful eye on your dog for signs of bloat at all times.

SOCIALIZATION

Most breeders recommend early socialization and training. Get your dog used to such things as nail grinding or trimming, vacuuming of the coat, riding in the car, and getting a bath from the time he is a pup. Trying to convince a full-grown Great Dane that these are wonderful new experiences can be more of a job than most people can handle. It is best to introduce such activities early and continuously throughout the growing period so that they do not come as a shock to an older dog.

EXERCISE

Pups need good steady exercise, but not too much exercise. One breeder compared hard exercise in pups to taking a toddler on a vigorous hike. They need consistent, easy play, a chance to move around and be social but never hard or prolonged jogs. Our breeders feel a pup should be at least five months old before any serious exercise program is begun. Start easy at first, gradually building over the next year or so. A Great Dane is not mature until he is eighteen months to two years old and an all-out, vigorous exercise program should never be attempted until that time.

The key to good exercise is to do approximately the same amount of exercise each day, *never* letting the dog sit all week and then taking him for a long hard run on the weekend. A long vigorous walk or a time to play in the park is sufficient even for an apartment dog. One breeder feels it is very important to let him cool down (just as you would do after a workout) before you put him away to nap.

Show dogs need to be in good condition. Hard, well defined muscles are appealing to judges. As a working dog, the Great Dane should appear fit, not flabby. Because most dogs exercise best at a steady medium trot, a bicycle may be necessary. The average terrier can travel at a brisk trot next to a human who is walking fast or doing a slow jog. The problem with a Great Dane is that he will be walking if you are walking, and barely trotting if you are jogging. A bicycle at a slow steady pace is an excellent choice frequently used by show kennels and pet owners alike. Even for show dogs, thirty minutes is maximum for the day, preferably done ten to fifteen minutes out, resting for ten minutes, and then ten to fifteen minutes back. The dog should always be allowed to travel at a natural gait, never pushing for speed which is uncomfortable for him. Pets do not need that kind of vigorous exercise.

FENCING

Danes are basically easy to contain because they learn a lesson and remember it well. One breeder says she keeps her pups out of the garden with the use of an electric wire such as that which is used for cattle fencing. She says her Danes seldom hit the wire more than once, and that once the dogs are trained, the fence can be turned off and they will respect a single strand of wire for the rest of their lives. She reports that she once moved with several full grown Great Danes. The dog fencing could not be put up for a week and she kept the dogs contained in the interim by a single wire.

An exercise pen, while not advised for daily use, can be used to contain the dog if you are traveling. These four by four foot panels can be set up outside a motel or if you need to contain the dog for a short, supervised time, and work well especially if the dog has learned to stay in an X-pen from the time he is young. Danes do not climb or dig by nature and so they can sometimes be housed for a short time in ridiculously low fencing.

Please note that these are emergency or short-term solutions; for continuous use, or outside unsupervised play, all of our breeders recommend good, secure fencing. An outdoor run will need to be six feet tall and of strong material. Although Danes are not destructive like some working breeds, and they do not become bored and restless like some active breeds, they are large. Because of their size, it is easy for them to snap inexpensive chain link. Be sure the gauge of fencing is sufficient to contain the dog if he begins to lean or scratch.

Great Danes are usually happy to share their homes and lives with other pets.

In the long run, it is less expensive to buy good fencing to begin with than to have to patch or replace fencing every year. Runs should be a minimum of six to eight feet wide so the dog doesn't bang his tail and thirty feet long so he can be active. A standard four by eight foot run is barely large enough for the dog to turn around and gives him no room for exercise.

TRAINING

*I*f you are going to own a Great Dane, take on the responsibility of training him from the beginning. As a responsible member of the community, it is your duty to be sure your dog does not contribute to a negative image of the breed. No matter how nice the temperament, the Great Dane is a large dog and without proper training and socialization, may be difficult to contain. The mental health of your dog depends on the type and consistency of training you put into him. As with a child, you are molding his character. To a large extent, how well he fits into your family and how well he is accepted by your neighbors when he is an adult depends on the values you instill in him as a puppy and young adult.

Time is a necessary ingredient. If you turn him out in a run or in the backyard and never have time for him, he will become wild and uncontrollable. Great Danes love their families and need time to develop a bond. Quality time is no substitute for quantity! Though the quality of the time you spend with him is important, you also need to be sure there is enough of it so he does not feel alone.

Never try to physically dominate a Great Dane. To begin with, it is almost impossible. Never lose your temper. A house dog knows every inflection of his master's voice. Great Danes do best with motivational training, in short, frequent sessions and a variety of tasks which are interesting and challenging to the dog. It is important to establish limits early. Be clear in your expectations. If you have never raised a pup before, an obedience class may be helpful once he is about seven to ten months old; his immune system is developed and he has enough maturity to get through a class which is generally about an hour long. Young pups have very short attention spans, and putting them in a class too early only teaches them not to pay attention.

One breeder writes that the key to training a Great Dane is "Praise — Persistence — Patience." Be sure the early experiences are positive. If a Great Dane is teased by children, for example, he may not be tolerant of them later in his life. This is not the result of poor breeding or temperament, but a learned and developed behavior which is the natural product of poor experiences in the dog's early life.

The dam begins the puppy's training in the whelping box. When she is displeased with his behavior she will growl, shoving him with her muzzle and rolling him onto his back (the submissive behavior for dogs) or snapping at him if the behavior continues. Like his mother, a voice of displeasure, a sharply barked command, or a stern verbal reprimand will produce the desired effect in most cases. Begin with the command "NO," which roughly translates, "Whatever you are doing, stop it!" In some cases, your pup may already have a rough knowledge of that command by the time he arrives at your home, which he has developed through contact with his breeder. If not, be sure it is the first thing you teach him.

House manners must be established early, as living with an unruly full-size Great Dane is simply not a pleasure. Set the rules and be consistent. If he finds that he can put his feet up on the chair one day but not the next, it will only encourage him to keep testing you. When he does what you want, always be sure to praise him.

Remember, never let a puppy do anything you do not want a full-grown Great Dane to do. Behaviors which are cute on a Miniature Pinscher, or even a Cocker Spaniel may not be as cute in a one hundred and sixty pound dog. Jumping up to say "Hello" is an example. Discourage these behaviors while the puppy is young with firm, immediate correction. One breeder says that if you take a puppy into bed with you to quiet him, you may have the dog in the bed for the rest of his life. Don't count on the fact that he will become discouraged about the furniture when he gets too large for it. Danes are remarkably good at finding a way to fit. Even chairs are not exempt. It is common to see a Great Dane sitting in a chair with his front feet on the ground.

Breeders differ on discipline. Some think that a smack on the bottom is better than a finger on the nose, believing that a rap on the nose will make the dog hand shy. Other breeders think that Great Danes are not naturally prone to be hand shy, and say they don't think a Great Dane can even feel a slap on the bottom — that your hand will suffer long before the dog will. Talk to your breeder before your pup comes home as to how to handle rules and discipline. It is best to continue with the technique used by the breeder, especially for the first month or so until the pup develops and matures a little. In any case, the command and the reprimand should be short, firm and non-abusive. The idea is to stop the undesirable behavior, not to intimidate the dog.

Firm verbal commands and consistent, fair treatment should be the goal. People who are confident and stable in their own personalities will raise a dog which is confident and stable. Constant nagging and drawn out punishment only confuses a dog. Remember, that in order to make him want to please you, he must KNOW when he pleases you. Praise is an important and necessary ingredient.

This undermarked Harlequin does not have an acceptable show color, but he can be a lovely pet and can even show in obedience trials.

One trick is to outmaneuver the dog so that you never get into direct confrontation. Switching a favorite toy for a shoe you do not wish the puppy to chew gives you the shoe, and keeps you from simply pulling it away from him. Without trading the shoe for a toy the puppy will feel that the shoe is a prize, and he will try to take it back as a natural reaction. Or, he may mistake your action for a game. Great Danes love to play games and he will naturally try to take it back. If you say "NO," take the shoe and give him the toy, he will learn the lesson, and be sidetracked to the toy, instead of concentrating on getting the prize back. The same is true for chasing the pup if he has something you don't want him to have. Danes love to play chase, and will only be encouraged to take the item whenever he can so that the game can begin.

Generally a short, sharp command such as "No," "Leave it," or "Stop" should be taught. It means everything from "don't eat that," to "don't chase the cat," to "stop chewing the electric cord."

Learning his name is another early lesson. The puppy has probably learned to come to a general puppy call for food, or to come in for the evening. Simply continue that by calling his name when you feed him. Although some breeders do not believe in treats to reward behavior, many of our breeders feel that this is a perfectly natural and acceptable practice. As long as the treat is accepted with proper control, not snapped out of the hand, it seems reasonable to many that the dog should get a reward for proper behavior.

Next, a puppy should learn to walk on a leash early in his life. The idea of trying to leash train a full-grown Great Dane is much more absurd than trying to leash train a full-grown Toy Poodle for example! Wait to put a collar on him until after his ears are healed and no longer bothering him, because pups tend to scratch at a collar at first, and there is a danger that tender, newly healed skin will be damaged. The surgery should be healed, but you do not need to wait until the ears are fully standing and completely out of tape before you begin.

Put the collar on the puppy and simply let him walk around. Some puppies will be convinced that they cannot move another inch until the collar comes off, while others are not concerned in the slightest and take little notice of what is hanging around their neck. Attach the leash, and simply follow the dog around for a while, going where he wants to go. Make it a

game to begin with. You can increase your command over the situation by talking, playing or offering a treat to change the puppy's direction, or to make him follow you. Be sure that the lessons are short, and that he can always succeed in achieving what you want to teach him that day. Never quit on a bad note, but don't continue to fight a losing fight. If he will not follow you, reconstruct the exercise so that you are asking him to do something you can get him to do. Then praise his efforts and quit for the day. Always break the task down into small parts that he can understand and make it as fun as possible for a very young puppy.

When the pup gets used to the leash, a choke collar can be used. *Never leave a choke collar on the dog when you are not with him as it can catch on things and the dog can be choked, injured or even killed.* Be firm in *how* he walks. Use the choke collar to give him a short, sharp correction when he begins to pull. Our breeders fell there is nothing more disturbing than being pulled down the street by a full-grown Great Dane. Remember, it takes two to pull. If he begins to lean into the leash, bring him back to your side, verbally correct him, and *let slack back into the leash.* If he takes it out, repeat the process, but never get into the situation where you are allowing him to lean against the leash. By the time he is fully grown you will be flying down the street behind him, out of control or being dragged like a plow if you don't put an early stop to such behavior.

Another habit you will have to decide about is mouthing. Many breeds have a tendency to approach a loved one and to take the hand or arm in their mouths. Great Dane pups tend to be quite playful — and this play often involves mouthing. It begins with playful puppy biting, and the puppy's natural inclination — like a human baby — is to test the environment by gripping and holding. It is important to teach the pup the limits to this kind of playing and roughhousing. It is all right as long as the pup stops when you want him to stop. Use of a key word spoken in an authoritative voice and possibly the use of a correction like popping him on the nose while saying "stop," or "no," will help train the pup. As noted, it is a natural instinct with Great Danes to use mouthing as a sign of affection and you may want to consider that it is his form of hugging before you become too alarmed. Just be very sure that the mouthing stays benign and loving, never rough or aggressive.

By the time he is ready for obedience classes, he should have some understanding of basic commands such as his name, "No," how to walk on a leash, and how to know when you are pleased and when you are not pleased. If you have taken him out and about on a regular basis, the noise, confusion and other dogs in the obedience class should not frighten him. Obedience classes in some areas of the country are crowded, and there may be a waiting list. Breeders often recommend that you investigate these classes immediately upon purchasing a puppy so that you will be at the top of the waiting list by the time the puppy is ready to begin more formal training. Remember, however, that Danes are large and perfection is sometimes very hard to achieve. Stop when they get it right, even if it is the first time. Continued practice can discourage a Dane rather than perfect his performance.

Socialization is important. Vary the places you take him and frequently introduce him to new people. By nature, Great Danes like new situations and meeting people. Shopping centers or parks are great adventures, with a lot of noise and strange sights and smells. If you begin to take him out early, he will develop self-confidence. People are attracted to these giants because they are elegant and gentle. Tell strangers the dog's name and encourage them to pet the dog and talk to him. If your pup does act shy or spooky at something, *don't encourage that behavior by reassuring him that "it's OK."* This is one of the most common mistakes made by new owners who are trying to be kind to their dogs. If he shies away from someone or something, and you pat him and tell him it is all right, he does not make the connection that the situation is all right, he makes the connection that his behavior is acceptable and will be encouraged to repeat it. Be firm. Make him approach the object or person, or at least stand while the person approaches or you bring the item close to him. Be slow about forcing him, but be firm and do not let him bolt.

As discussed in the health chapter, the developmental stages of a Great Dane, especially between seven and nine months and again between fourteen and eighteen months, may lead to a sudden change of personality. Especially around nine months the dog may become shy and spooky at situations which have never bothered him before. He suddenly notices things he has not seen or not paid attention to before. If

this happens, make an extra effort to get him to some kind of class, either obedience or conformation, so that he can again become confident in strange situations. This stage will pass, especially if you work with him and do not encourage shy behavior with pats and reassurance.

As they reach sexual maturity, you may encounter a period when males who have been well housetrained want to lift their leg and "mark" their territory. Be quick and firm to discourage this behavior. A sharp word and confining him to a crate or putting him outside should suffice and the stage will pass. Be especially firm and consistent about house behavior at this time. This teenage stage can be as trying in dogs as it is in children. The dog will often test to see what he can get away with. If you have established rules and been firm and consistent about them when he was a pup, it will be easier to get through this stage with a well behaved dog. Bitches will also go through this stage but usually not to the same extent.

Never encourage aggression with commands like, "Sic him," or "Go get him." A Great Dane will guard your home and his family by nature. He does not need encouragement. If you continually encourage aggressive behavior at the whim of the dog, you will be laying the groundwork for a potentially dangerous situation. These gentle giants are not aggressive by nature, though they will bark at intruders. To make them aggressive through training is a travesty. None of our breeders want to see their dogs go into homes where aggression was encouraged to the point where the dog would eventually be placed in a situation where he could be considered aggressive, out of control or dangerous. In any situation where the dog makes an error in judgment about when and under what circumstances to attack, it is the dog who suffers, in some cases with his life!!

SHIPPING AND TRAVEL

*I*f you do not find a puppy locally that is right for you and your family, you may have to buy one from out of the area. If the pup is young, it is not a problem to fly him. Flying a full-grown Great Dane does pose more of a problem. If you have a choice of driving eight or ten hours or flying a puppy, flying is an option to consider. Although some of our breeders are very much against flying, many report that puppies travel very well. Several indicate that they feel a flight causes less stress on the pup, who usually goes to sleep with the sound of the engines, than a long car trip. Car trips can stress a pup because of temperature and water changes, strange potty stops where the pup may be exposed to viruses, lack of exercise and motion which may cause car sickness. It is very common for pups to get car sick but not air sick. Great Danes are more likely to have a problem with one of these elements of driving than with a flight. Although there are some stories of dogs being mishandled or dying during shipping, one breeder says she has shipped dogs over half of a million air miles over the years, and has never had a problem. We could not find a single breeder who had directly had a real trauma with airlines. While some breeds of dogs have breathing or respiration problems which make them poor shipping risks, Great Danes will generally settle in for the ride and enjoy the experience.

Flying a puppy in is relatively easy. A puppy may not fly until it is eight weeks old. Shipping should take place after the first set of shots have been given. The cost is usually $100-$140 for the flight, and $45-$65 for the crate. A dog may not ship if the temperature is below 30 degrees, or higher than 90 degrees. If the pup goes freight, you may pay for the flight and even the crate (if you purchase it from the airlines) collect, at the time you pick up your pup at the airport. Airlines use a top-of-the-line crate but there are several good, less expensive crates on the market which are still safe and airline approved, but at half the cost. This crate will only be useful for a puppy, since a full-grown Great Dane will need a much larger crate. Since airline freight is figured by volume, as well as weight, you do not want to fly him in a crate which is larger than he needs because it will double or even triple the price. Also, the pup will be more comfortable in something which is small and cave-like and where he will not be thrown back and forth with the movement of the crate. The breeder will drop off the puppy at his local freight office of the airline, and you will pick him up at the same office in your town. Dogs may not travel on trains.

If you have picked up your pup at the airport, bring him directly home; do not use that opportunity to visit friends and show him off. He needs to see his new home, have time and quiet to get adjusted, and to get food and water. Although the airlines require food and water dishes, most breeders will not send food or water with the pup. A full stomach can lead to airsickness, and water bowls tip as the crate is carried and leave the bedding wet and cold. Bring the pup home, let him inspect the new area, and give him a bed, food and water immediately. With a full stomach and a little quiet, he will begin to adjust in a short time. Don't expect him to be confident and completely comfortable right away. It will probably take a day or two for him to settle in and become the normal, active puppy he was when he left his litter.

Flying a Great Dane is more difficult than flying a smaller dog. Smaller breeds can fly with passengers as excess baggage and are checked in at the main airline counter, and picked up at the baggage carousel like skis or golf clubs. A Great Dane needs a very large crate, and will usually have to be checked in at the freight department. Although you can fly a dog in a wire crate, owners who frequently ship Great Danes often buy a special aluminum crate which is custom made for the large dogs These will last forever, but they are an investment of $500 or more. For that reason, bitches being bred to dogs out of the area often make use of frozen semen, which can go in overnight mail or ship counter to counter as medical supplies.

Great Danes adapt easily to new places if they have been raised properly, and they can become good, solid travelers. They travel well in motor homes for a change-of-pace family vacation, and Great Danes will usually be happy to see new surroundings and take long hikes in the wilderness after you arrive. A walk in a new city can also be of interest to them.

If you are traveling by car with a puppy, take a few precautions to help make the trip easier. Do not feed him for an hour or so before you leave. One breeder suggests feeding the pup a couple of ginger snaps before travel to help prevent carsickness. (Pups who get carsick generally outgrow it by the time they are six months old.) Take him for a walk right before departure so that he has every opportunity to relieve himself while he still has the chance. Take along a box, bed or cage that he is used to so that something familiar will accompany him, much like bringing along a stuffed animal or blanket for a child. Don't let him travel with his head out of the window, as he can get grit or wind in his eyes. And, it is unsafe because he does not realize how fast the car is traveling and he may suddenly try to jump out. Stop every few hours to let him get a drink of water, get some exercise and relieve himself. Be sure to keep him on a leash so that he does not dart out in front of a car or approach a strange dog.

Never let your pup approach a strange dog. Although Great Danes are seldom aggressive to other dogs, the strange dog may attack too quickly for you to prevent serious injury to the puppy.

If you are traveling with your dog, be sure to bring plenty of food and water, bowls for food and water, and a leash. Even a dog that stays around the house is likely to become excited and disoriented in a strange place, and a leash is good insurance to keep him from wandering into traffic or getting lost. Other helpful items to travel with are Pepto Bismol tablets in case he eats something that gives him diarrhea, Dramamine for carsickness (especially if it is a young dog who has not ridden in a car often), Benadryl for insect bites, and flea spray, especially if you are near the beach. Having these things with you when you need them can be especially helpful and take some of the stress out of travel.

If you are using hotels, most of our breeders offered one word of advice: CRATE. Crate train your dog, and bring the crate on vacation with you. Some hotels will accept a crated dog, while they have learned not to accept dogs which may be left on their own in hotel rooms, bored, upset, and ready to do damage that these perfect pets would never think of doing at home. A crate is not punishment to a dog. For him, it is a part of his home which has come with him and gives him a feeling of stability. The crate can help him stay calm, and get some sleep while you go out to dinner or to see sights where a dog may not be allowed. A hotel room with a crate is certainly safer and better than locking him in a car.

In the hot weather, a crate is a necessity. **Never** leave a dog in the car, but if you are going somewhere such as a picnic or a baseball game, take the crate out of the car, place it in the shade, and the dog can safely be left without worrying about over heating. Heat stroke is one of the leading causes of death in well loved dogs — be careful during summer months.

Great Danes enjoy outdoor activities if they are with their humans, but they do not tolerate either extreme in temperature. Like most black dogs, Black Danes are especially sensitive to heat stroke. Their short coat and lean body build does not give them much protection in cold. They are better off inside during the heat of summer or the cold of winter.

If you are traveling and intend to leave the dog at home, there are three choices. You can kennel your dog, leave him in the care of a friend or relative, or set up some kind of care for him at your home. A kennel is the safest and easiest way to care for your dog when you are away, but many of our breeders advise that the Dane will often refuse to eat in a strange environment, and they worried about the stress bringing on bloat. Some of our breeders advise leaving the dog with family or friends, but that situation is not always possible. Having family or friends come to your house may also be a problem, since the dog must feel at home with the new baby-sitters. The hardy souls who volunteer to pet-sit for you should be used to giant dogs, and know what they are getting into.

If you are counting on someone coming into the house to feed and care for him, be sure that they are reliable. Friends or sitters who are not well recommended may be too busy to come by on a regular basis, and the dog may be at risk because if something goes wrong, it may go undetected. Since bloat needs to be spotted and treated immediately, a once-a-day visit from the caretaker is not sufficient.

Many areas of the country have professional "pet sitters." These people come into the home, check on pets and care for them, and keep an eye on the house at the same time. Professional pet sitters offer the advantage of keeping the dog at home where he feels comfort-

able, and at the same time, there is someone in and out of the house, and the dog is there to watch out for intruders. Even with a professional pet sitting service, be sure whoever is watching the dog is familiar with the signs of bloat and that they see the dog more than once a day.

The success of any pet sitting plan also depends the security of your yard (or the area where the dog is to be housed). If there is a yard or pool man going in or out, for example, there is a possibility the dog will slip out. If the fencing is not secure, or the shelter not good, pet sitting is not a good alternative.

BREEDING YOUR DOG —
WHY THIS MIGHT NOT BE SUCH A GOOD IDEA!

*N*ow that you have your dog, you may entertain the idea that you should breed it. If you read one of the larger books on the breed, or one of the many dog books that promotes breeding, it will discuss genetics and how to build a whelping box, and will make it sound easy. On the other hand, breeders and breed associations will say that you "should not breed your dog." That makes it sound like an ethical decision on a higher plane, and you may be tempted to simply say, "But I want just one litter, what could it hurt?" Here is probably the most honest evaluation of why this may be one of the many times in life when something LOOKS better on the outside than it does when you actually TRY it.

Have you ever gone somewhere and seen a WONDERFUL layout of model trains or a large doll house? It looked easy and the hobby looked fascinating. You may have even gone home and bought a small doll house, or a starter set of trains. Then you began to discover just how much time and money really went into this simple looking project. You needed space to work on the project, and space to set it up. You needed special tools and materials you had never worked with before, and they were all expensive. You had to spend time shopping for the right pieces of the right size so that it all went together. And they were expensive. Very quickly you found that this seemingly simple setup was going to cost you hours and hours of your life and hundreds of dollars just to get off to a good start. And when you put together the first pieces, it was a boring, poor substitute for the intricate, fascinating setup you had seen. In the end you gave up on it, losing what money you might have invested in the train set which is now on a shelf in the garage, or the doll house which still remains without those hundreds of maddening little shingles pasted to the roof! In short, your time and money were not well spent unless you found it to be something you were interested in to the point where you became involved and dedicated!

Like all hobbies, there is much more to dog breeding than first meets the eye. Enthusiasts put time and money into this, just as with any hobby. And the result which looks simple is the product of careful planning and investment. To do it in any way short of that kind of planning will result in something far short of the goal, which is a waste of your time and money. Even a single litter can consume much more time and money than you ever imagined when you began the project.

In 1995, 3,247 *litters* of Great Danes were registered with AKC. This is up from 1994, when 2,955 litters were registered. There were 11,015 individual dogs registered in 1995. This means there were only about four pups from each litter registered, although our breeders report that an average litter is nine or ten pups. This means that there are about twice as many Great Danes whelped every year as are registered. These "left over" dogs usually go to pet homes, and often the owners never bother to register them. Some of them will find their way into the breeding population, being bred to local dogs, to produce low quality Great Danes, which will find their way into the local newspapers. With that kind of population, it is no wonder that the breed has suffered in quality, health and temperament. All Great Danes are simply NOT alike!

Most people decide to breed their dog for one of the following reasons:

A) It looks like easy money. Call a few breeders, find out the price of pups, and the number of pups in a litter, and the profit doesn't look bad. But remember, you are playing the *Kibbles and Bits Slot Machine*. You may make money on a litter here and there, but there is a greater potential to lose money, sanity, friends and routine. The odds are better at Las Vegas. How much stress is it worth to you to make a few dollars? How many nice things in your home will end up with tooth marks? And like any new business venture, there is ALWAYS investment before there is profit. How much are you willing to invest before you have a payoff?

B) People think that it would be a wonderful experience for the children. Buy a video! It's cheaper, cleaner, less stressful, and the kids will learn more. The kids will play with the pups for a few days and then go back to Nintendo or outside to play ball, depending on their interests. A litter of eight-week-old pups is too young to have manners enough to stay away from Nintendo controls, but too small to play outside with the kids! In the end, the kids may find the pups more annoying than interesting. It is like having eight toddlers around the house. One of our breeders says she remembers her children taking the pups out of the puppy pen, then getting interested in something else and forgetting about the pups, leaving unhousetrained pups prying into every corner of the house unsupervised! Great Dane pups are born at about a pound, but grow rapidly. By the time they are able to move around at four or five weeks old, they are large enough that nine or ten of them can create not only a mess in terms of what they can get into and what they are strong enough to pull and chew, but they can also generate several pounds of waste in a very short period of time.

C) You may decide you want a second dog. Friends and family have said they also wanted a dog. But frequently, friends who have repeatedly said, "If you ever breed Hilda, we want a pup" will be the first to tell you AFTER the litter is eight weeks old and you have asked them when they are going to get their puppy that they "...really can't take a puppy this time, but for sure the next time you breed her!"

D) There may be no decision at all. A neighborhood male jumps the fence. (Yes, even six footers have been known to be scaled.) The bitch slipped out past the kids when she was in season. No one realized that she was in season. The list goes on and on. It is much easier to get an accidental breeding than you can ever imagine. Mixed litters are the hardest to get rid of, and you have all the disadvantages of raising a litter, with none of the advantages of producing a nice puppy, or being able to sell it. For this reason, we highly recommend that you SPAY ANY BITCH YOU DID NOT BUY FOR THE EXPRESS PURPOSE OF BREEDING.

If you bought your dog as a pet, you may find that you have a limited registration, which means that your pups are not eligible for registration. The breeder, with his working knowledge of genetics, may have priced your dog as a pet and found a pet home for her because for some reason he did not feel that puppies should be produced from her.

When you consider breeding your dog, think about some very important factors. One of the reasons why Great Danes are not as overbred as some breeds, such as Cocker Spaniels, is that they are difficult to breed. From the onset of the physical breeding to caring for ten, large and rapidly growing puppies, breeding is a huge investment in time, money and space.

First, did you buy a nice quality dog, from a good breeder? Is this a dog the breeder himself would want to breed? If the answer is "NO," don't breed your dog just to get a litter of puppies. This kind of breeding lowers the quality of the Great Dane, and gives the breed a bad name. If you did not make it clear that you were looking for a breeding bitch at the time of purchase, the chances are that your bitch is not of breeding quality. This goes back to the necessity of making it very clear WHAT you want the dog for at the time of purchase, and being willing to pay a good price for good quality. There may be hidden genetic problems that the breeder knows are in your dog — ones that will not affect her life and health, but which may appear in her puppies. The breeder may not have explained this to you because you said all you wanted was a pet. As long as YOUR dog was not affected, there was no reason for the breeder to go into it. But if you breed the dog, the problem will surely appear again, and then YOU are the breeder who has to deal with the problem. You are the one who has to deal with puppy buyers upset over problems with their puppies. You are the one who must agree to replace a puppy that has a problem, or be prepared and knowledgeable enough to help the new owner cope with the situation.

Second, even though there are a lot of dogs in the newspaper every week, remember that with all of the Great Danes out there, it may not be as easy as it looks to sell the pups. It is one thing to look at a litter of nine pups and say to yourself, "Even at $200 each, that is $1,800!" and another to reap that kind of profit. It may sound like a jackpot. You appear to do nothing, and extra pocket money comes rolling in! But think about the expenses you incur. The road is filled with pitfalls, chewed furniture, expenses that add up like a city street repair budget, and more work than being coach of the Little League team!

There is the expense and trouble of the breeding. Either one pup or a stud fee is usually paid to the owner of the stud, even if he is a local dog. Stud fees on known dogs run around $500 to $1,000. If you have chosen a dog that is not within driving distance, you will need to ship the bitch or the semen. Shipping the frozen semen is easier, but then you must pay a vet, or someone who is authorized to make the breeding to inseminate the bitch.

If you are breeding to a good stud, you will have to plan ahead to book the breeding. It is best to prepare for the breeding BEFORE the bitch comes in season. You will need to send a copy of your bitch's pedigree and perhaps her picture to the owner of the stud for approval in most cases. When it is time for breeding, you will have to get a current brucellosis test. Although uncommon, brucellosis is a contagious disease which is usually sexually transmitted between dogs. It can be contagious to humans from handling the dogs during breeding or whelping, and there is some new evidence to show it can also be transmitted between dogs through waste material. Rather than risk it, most breeders will require a current brucellosis certificate. A test from six months or a year before is not considered current. Many breeders will also require hip and eye certification. These tests can eat up the price of two to three more pups.

You have to build or buy a box for her to whelp and raise the pups or she will pick the bed, a closet (after she has pulled all of the clothes off the hangers to make her own bed) or the middle of the flower bed. Pups need shots and worming. Even if your vet is very reasonable, $65 is the lowest you will pay, ($25 for the office call and $5 per pup). And it is time consuming to take the pups to the vet. You have the expense of the puppy food, and the additional food the bitch will require during the time she is carrying and nursing. Eight to ten pups will consume an alarming amount of food. You will have to be able to watch and spot growth problems in individual pups and know what to do when, not if, they develop.

You will have to decide what you will do about ear cropping. Uncropped Danes are sometimes *very* hard to sell, since almost everyone associates cropped ears with the breed. Ear cropping will frequently run $100 to $200 for each pup. There is also the time involved in ear care, and you will have to know something about taping the ears in order to replace the dressing and keep the ears clean and erect during those first critical few weeks. These expenses must be paid before the pups are sold.

Advertising in the local newspaper will run at least $20 to $40 per weekend. Count the number of Great Dane ads in your newspaper. The odds are that you will not be able to sell the entire litter in one weekend. It will take you three or four AT BEST. You will have to stay home to answer the phone, and you will have at least a dozen strangers coming to your home to see the pups. Great Danes are cute pups and there are the inevitable "window shoppers." The price of two or three pups will be needed JUST TO COVER THE EXPENSE YOU HAVE IN RAISING THE LITTER AND SELLING IT.

There are often problems with a sale. Someone buys a pup, and it gets sick, and they want YOU to pay the vet bill. Or they can't keep it and want to bring it back. Someone brings in a virus and the litter gets sick and you have hundreds of dollars of vet bills — it happens all the time. Even the best breeders have problems with a virus in a litter from time to time.

As the pups begin to move around, they may get out of their area and chew up furniture or kitchen cabinets. The force of a litter of wiggling, happy, uncontrollable seven-week-old puppies is enough to move such things as baby gates and temporary pens, and scratch up back doors. Outside, these little fellows will dig and chew up bushes unless you have a specific pen built for them. Now we are into the expense of building a place to contain them between the time the bitch has had enough, and when you can sell them. This could be the longest month of your life! You must think of a way to begin to house train the litter, and spend the time to socialize them so that people coming to look at the pups are not met with wild pups, unused to human handling.

And winter puppies, inside because of the cold weather, will shred papers, take down barriers, and create literally several pounds of wet and soiled papers a day. Mopping and scraping smeared puppy poop will become a way of life! Certainly there are crates and cages called "puppy play pens" which do a very good job containing puppies and eliminating some of the mess. But they will run in the neighborhood of $140 each and will take up a space of about 4' X 4' in some inconvenient place in your home! You will need two for a litter of eight pups. In addition, they have wire floors which splay feet and break down the pasterns of heavy Great Dane pups.

In short, many people breed a litter because they think it is easy money, they want the "experience" of having a litter (which is a little like wanting to have the experience of juggling eight bowling balls without dropping them on your foot!), or they want the kids to have the fun of a litter. They may want a second dog and this looks like a way to get one for themselves, friends, or family members.

By the time you add up expenses, it is cheaper to simply buy a nice second dog, and let your friends and relatives do the same. If they like your dog, give them the name of your breeder! One puppy is fun, two are a chore, and four or more can be overwhelming if you are not set up for it, and if you do not have the time to devote to it. Eight can be a disaster. Breeders do this as a hobby. It interests them, they have invested time and money — just as you would with any hobby that interests you — in finding the best way to handle pups. Every one of them has early disaster stories to tell.

Perhaps this is the time to mention that the odor of your home may change, and friends may be less inclined to visit. Whelping has a distinctive smell. Amniotic fluid is dark green, stains whatever it comes in contact with, and has a permeating fragrance. Although the bitch will clean up after the litter when they are very young, her housekeeping may be somewhat lax when they get older and start on solid food. One of our breeders says she bought a breadmaking machine so that the aroma of yeast and fresh bread would fill the house, instead of the aroma of puppies!

Time is another thing you will need. When it is time to breed your bitch, you will need to drop everything and get it done. Putting it off until the weekend will often be too late. Veterinarians are often way off in their predictions of when to breed. They go by the book, and the bitch has not read it! Keep in close contact with your breeder, who knows what to expect, and make arrangements as soon as possible using his guidelines. If neither you nor the stud owner know what you are doing, be warned that Great Danes are a giant breed and sometimes difficult to handle during breeding. Injury to either the dog or bitch is a constant possibility if the dogs are left to themselves. A "tie" may last several minutes to nearly an hour. A dog dismounting from a bitch without help can fall over backward, resulting in anything from a strained to a broken back. If the bitch drops or sits down, she can rupture herself or the male's penis. These are only a sampling of the problems, but it is sufficient to say that Danes have died due to injuries sustained during breeding. *Someone who is experienced in dog breeding should be present.* Problems may arise, someone must know what to do about them. Nature is not as reliable as you may imagine. At best, the breeding may not be successful, at worst, the dog or bitch may be injured or killed.

Are you prepared to stay home when the bitch is ready to whelp? Just as Murphy's Law predicts, the bitch is guaranteed to whelp in the middle of a dinner party, or on the day you have an important appointment — even if she has to be days early or days late to do it! The need of a Caesarean Section is always a possibility in Great Danes, and will be required in about 30% of the litters delivered. That leads to even more time and expense. Do you know the danger signals which indicate when a C-section is needed and do you have a vet on call who can handle an emergency surgery on a Great Dane? First time bitches are often poor or confused mothers who do not clean pups well, or who step on pups. You should always be present at a whelping, especially with a first time bitch, or risk losing pups and/or the dam. During whelping, which can take ten or twelve hours or more from start to finish, the bitch will need to relieve herself. She will have a discharge for over a week and your floors will need to be mopped several times a day. Get ready to buy stock in Clorox!

After they are born, you will need to start handling the pups from the beginning. The bitch will be exhausted for the first few days. (And we are not even going to get into the extra problems in caring for a litter delivered by C-section.) Even good mothers can injure pups unintentionally during the first forty-eight hours after whelping. A whelping box with "pig rails" (a ledge built out from the side of the pen which allows the pups to slip under them, but keeps the dam away from the edges of the box where she can crush the pups), will help, but it is advisable for someone to sleep close by to assist pups if necessary. Watch for poor nursers. Sometimes you will need to physically put a puppy on the teat and hold him on until he can get his fill if he is nursing slowly, or is getting shoved out of the way in a big litter. And there is always the chance that one or more of the pups will need tube or bottle feeding at least as a supplement. You don't want to do this? You think nature can simply take its course? Be prepared to lose pups, sometimes half the litter or more.

There is the time you will need to take them to the veterinarian for shots. Call your vet before you breed and ask what he charges to worm and give shots to a large litter. This alone may shock you. Remember, we have given minimum prices; many vets are much higher. There is the time you will need to spend with them just getting them used to people and being handled. You will need to educate yourself about early socialization training, such as rolling the pups on their back. (Do you know why this is appropriate? If not, consider it just one of the things you do not know and need to learn from an experienced breeder before you try breeding.)

And there is the inevitable cleanup time. When the litter gets older, they will be glad to try to help you with these chores by eating the mop, broom, or papers as you are trying to get the job done. This kind of help does not speed up the process. Pups need to be fed and cared for like babies, in the morning when you are late, and at night when you are tired. Ten Dane pups produce literally pounds of waste material a day, not counting the weight of wet paper. If you do not have space for them to get away from the poop, or if you fail to keep their pen clean (complete cleaning several times a day), they will learn to tolerate filth in spite of their natural aversion to it. Once that happens, neither you nor their new owner can count on their natural tendencies to aid in housetraining, and they are liable to be extremely difficult to train.

One breeder says, "The amazing thing about it is that when a mother sheep has baby sheep, the mother sheep takes care of them. When a mother horse has a baby horse, the mother horse takes care of it. But when a bitch whelps, YOU take care of them!"

Great Dane pups grow very rapidly. They are born at one to two pounds, which has doubled by the end of the first week. By three weeks of age, when their eyes are open and they begin to move around, they will weigh five to seven pounds. By the time they are two months old and ready to go to new homes, they will be nineteen to twenty-four pounds. That means that you will need to have housing, pens, and space for as much as two hundred and forty pounds of puppies! You will need a full room of your house dedicated to the litter. If you want to put them outside, remember that Great Dane pups are fairly delicate and will need a fully insulated, well ventilated shelter to keep them clean, dry and comfortable.

Finally, what will you do with the pups if you cannot sell them? Eight to ten puppies is a lot of puppies to sell. How long will you keep them? Will you take the responsibility of raising them until suitable homes can be found, or will you simply unload the remainder of the litter on the already overloaded animal shelters? Does your neighborhood have ordinances about the number of dogs you can keep, and how many puppies you can sell before you will be considered a business? What local laws are there in your area concerning your responsibility as the seller? Some states have passed a wide variety of laws within the last several years designed to discourage dog breeding and help eliminate the overflow of unwanted pets. Be sure to check into them before you breed.

If you truly are interested in breeding dogs, go to some shows, talk to breeders, do your homework for the next phase of your hobby, just as we have advised throughout this book. Decide what style of dog you want to breed, what temperament you feel a Great Dane should have, and what purpose you want your puppies to fill in their new homes. Consider that you will need to keep several pups from your first litters in order to see how well your breeding program is working. Do you have room for several Great Dane adults?   Do you have facilities to keep the dogs safe and confined away from each other if they do not get along?

Then, study the pedigrees to find out what bloodlines are most likely to produce the type of dog you want. Decide how you will determine if you are reaching your goal. Will you show them to check their conformation quality? Will you temperament test them, check on the pups after they have been placed in homes, or use them as therapy dogs? Will you train them as working dogs? What kind of homes will they fit into, and how will you sell them? What kind of guarantee will you offer new owners? Don't opt out and say, "Well, I'm only breeding pets." These dogs are taken into people's homes as family members. Most pet buyers are inexperienced and depend on the breeder to know what he or she is doing. Can you be happy simply walking away from a problem which crops up in one of your pups, or is that very much like consigning to another family problems you would not want in your own home?

What will you do when callers feel your price is too high? When you bred there may not have been more than one ad in the newspaper for Great Danes, but perhaps by the time your pups are ready there are three other ads and everyone is dropping their prices. How low will you drop your price? Or what if there are no calls at all? Summer is a good time to raise pups, but many people vacation and any breeder will tell you it is a very slow time to sell pups. By the time they are three months old, the pups are not as cute as they once were, and will weigh as much as fifty-five pounds each. It is easy to see how this project can become a nightmare if you do not have the time, dedication and facilities to care for several large dogs.

From a practical standpoint, how will you handle the litter? Look at facilities of other breeders. Ask what kinds of equipment you will need. Ask about vaccinations and ear care. Find a good vet who is familiar with the breed and willing to work with you. Do you have a vet who knows anything about whelping and caring for a litter? Where will you get help if something goes wrong? Do you have the time to socialize them, and a clear idea of how you will do it?

We strongly advise finding a breeder who is willing to work with you as a mentor. He has the experience you will need to tap into and can give you advice along the way if things don't go as planned.

After you have thought out the project completely, if you are sure this is what you want to do, begin to plan your first breeding well before it takes place. Like anything else, careful planning and forethought can save stress, money, grief and your home!

Some of our breeders recounted how they got started. For many, it was a matter of seeing a dog they liked, investigating his lines, and finding the right person to help and advise them. Then they invested as much money as they could afford in the best bitch they could find. Sometimes this worked, but many of our breeders reported starting again and again until they got the right foundation stock, clear of problems and representing the ideal they had in mind for the breed.

There is a lot more to breeding than owning a pet. If you intend to do it, be sure that you do it as well as you can. Striving for excellence will provide you with the best possible chance of producing quality puppies and happy new owners. If this is not the way you intend to pursue breeding, DON'T DO IT. Save yourself time, money and stress, and save the animal shelter system the burden of taking on yet another unwanted, improperly cared for litter!

SHOPPING ARCADE

THE FOLLOWING SECTION IS A SHOWCASE OF FINE COMPANIES WHO PRODUCE AND SELL PRODUCTS WHICH ARE OF INTEREST TO GREAT DANE OWNERS.

Many of these goods and services you will not find in the course of your normal shopping patterns. Those who are involved with dogs and dog shows are used to finding an abundance of these kinds of products at the many show vendors they see each weekend, but we know that many of our readers do not have the same opportunities. We hope that by presenting these companies to you here, it will make your life with your Great Dane a little richer and easier. Please feel free to write us and let us know how you feel about this section, or this book in general. We encourage your comments and would like to hear from you. If at any time after publication you cannot make contact with a company listed in this section, or a breeder listed in the breeder sections, please contact Dace Publishing to get an updated number.

DREAMIN' DOG

Design A   **Design B**   **Design C**   **Design D**

These delightful drawings which capture the Great Dane, are available in black, brindle or fawn for A or B; Fawn, Black, Brindle or Harlequin for C; and Harlequin only for D. Specify color of dog when ordering. Fawn will be sent if no color is specified.

> 0131 - Parchment stationery - 20 sheets/envelopes $8.00
> 0132 - Notecards - 6 cards and envelopes $6.00

Notecards are available with red border, green border or white embossed border. Specify when ordering.

VACATION WITH YOUR PET!

Almost 700 pages of hotels, including rates and phone numbers, where your pet is welcome. Travel tips and other useful information.
0231 $19.95

ANIMAL NUTRITION

You may be poisoning your pet, unknowingly, a little each day. John Rowe has compiled fifteen years of research to help you understand how and why your dog's health can be affected by what you feed him.
0232 $12.95

NATURAL, HOMEMADE LIVER SNACKS

Avoid snacks made of cereal and other fillers. Your Great Dane deserves and responds best to a dog's favorite food. These Liver based snacks are a delight to dogs and have been the secret of show, field and obedience kennels for years. Now available for the first time to owners who love their pets and want the best for them.

FOUR FABULOUS FLAVORS DOGS LOVE BEST:
GARLIC ~ MINT ~ PARSLEY ~ CARROT
(indicate flavor when ordering)

0701   Trial size, 6 oz....$3.50
0702   Regular size, 1 lb.......$7.95
0703   Economy size, Full 2 1/4 lbs!......$15.95

Convenient, easy training treats dogs love!

TO ORDER: Prices good through 6/98. After which call for availability and current pricing. Include full name and address, item number, quantity, design and/or color where necessary. If using VISA/MC, include number, cardholder name, and expiration date.

DREAMIN'DOG
P.O.7787
Charlottesville, VA 22906
(888)840-3223
VA res. add 4.5% sales tax

<u>Shipping/handling:</u>
Orders up to $15.00 add $3.75,
$15. - $50.00 add $4.75,
$50. - $100.00 add $5.75,
$100.- $200.00 add $6.75,
over $200.00 add $9.75

Gatekeepers Legend of Dakota, at 10 months, with the Seehof's grandaughter.
Dakota serves as a hearing dog for the Seehofs' friend.

All Gatekeeper Danes are guaranteed for hereditary defects.

Jerome and Olivia Seehof have a deep love of dogs, and that provides the motivating force behind their success. They have the experience of the past twenty five years of educating dog owners.

Gatekeeper kennel is dedicated to the future of the Great Dane breed, and each generation of their breeding program has shown the true merit of their contribution to this magnificent breed. Gatekeeper Danes consistently produces noble giants whose intelligence is superior, whose devotion is legendary, and whose gentleness is their legacy.

Gatekeeper Great Danes
20797 N. 30th Ave
Barryton, MI 49305
(517) 382-7420